THE DEMOCRATIC CONTROL OF WORK

"For shortness' sake, I will call it the idea of freedom"
— Theodore Parker

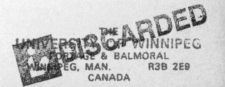

The Democratic Control of Work

or

a Panacea for the Ills of Society

by

ALASTAIR CAMPBELL

illustrated by
JOHN RYAN

sponsored by the
Scottish Co-operatives Development Committee

BETTER BUSINESS BETTER LIVING

PLUNKETT FOUNDATION
— FOR CO-OPERATIVE STUDIES —

ISBN 0 85042 082 2

First published in 1987 by the
PLUNKETT FOUNDATION FOR CO-OPERATIVE STUDIES
31 St. Giles'
Oxford OX1 3LF
England

Typeset by
Quadraset Limited, Midsomer Norton, Avon

Printed in Great Britain by
Antony Rowe Limited, Chippenham, Wiltshire

DEDICATION

I like the old fashioned idea of dedicating a book to some distinguished person. Accordingly I dedicate this book to the following people, listed in the order in which I met them -

Iain and **Rosie**, without whose inititial encouragement this book might never have been written.

David Spreckley and **Mike Campbell**, the Chairman and Secretary who welcomed me to Demintry, the forerunner of ICOM.

Roger Sawtell, the second Chairman of ICOM.

Antoine Antoni and **François Espagne**, the joint General Secretaries who welcomed me to SCOP in France.

Antonio Calleja*, the Director who welcomed me to the Management Division of Lan Kide Avrreskia in Mondragon.

Robert Oakeshott, the founder of JOL.

George Benello and **David Ellerman**, the Americans who welcomed me respectively to FED &the forerunner of AWD) and to the ICA.

Kai Blomquist, the Secretary who welcomed me to the Cooperativa Institutet of Sweden.

Bohdan Trampczynski, who welcomed me to the CZSP in Poland, of which organisation he was for over 20 years the elected leader.

Cairns Campbell, the first Director of the SCDC in Scotland.

ICOM = Industrial Common Ownership Movement
SCOP = Sociétés Co-operatives Ouvrières de Production
JOL = Job Ownership Ltd
FED = Federation for Economic Democracy
AWD = Association for Workplace Democracy
ICA = Industrial Co-operative Association
CZSP = Centralny Zwiazek Spókdzielczości Pracy
SCDC = Scottish Co-operatives Development Committee

* a shortened version of his name.

v

There is nothing,
more difficult to achieve,
more perilous to conduct,
nor more uncertain of success,
than to initiate a new order of things.

For the innovator has for enemies
all those who benefited under the old order
and hence would not change,
and only lukewarm supporters
amongst those who would benefit from the new.

This coolness arises
partly from the incredulity of mankind,
who do not truly believe in anything new
until they have had long and successful experience of it.

— Machiavelli

CONTENTS

Introduction

A — Practical Demonstration

"New opinions are always suspect, and usually opposed, without any other reason than because they are not already common" — John Locke

The theme of this book is that the conventional system of (private or public) capital ownership of industry — which means control of work by capital — is an anachronism. It was a satisfactory system before the industrial revolution: but it is quite inappropriate to the conditions of work which now obtain in the industrialised Western democracies.

We thus waste our time trying to improve it. We must face the fact that we have to abandon capital ownership and substitute a system of worker-ownership of business enterprises. This is an immense change which will transform industry and society: but we can bring it about quietly and gradually one business at a time.

Experiments in worker-ownership have taken place all over the world. Unfortunately the idea of having work controlled by people at work usually gets mixed up with other social and political aims: so that the failure of most of these efforts is no evidence that the theory of worker-ownership of business enterprises is impractical. Furthermore there are two areas in Europe in which it has become an established success. The organisations there clearly demonstrate its practicality. They also provide us with a blueprint of how to do it.

The existence of the Mondragon group of worker-owned enterprises in the Basque province of Spain is now quite well known. It comprises some 20,000 people operating more than 100 businesses with established success. What is hardly known at all, however, is that over two million people are operating in almost exactly the same way in Poland, Czechoslovakia, Hungary and Romania. Although economic conditions behind the Iron Curtain are obviously not the same as those in Spain, the methods of operating worker-ownership there are so similar to those of Mondragon that a coherent pattern appears. It is interesting that the authorities on both sides of the Iron Curtain started by ignoring their embryo worker-ownership movements, on the grounds that they would never come to anything. Details of (what are now) these large and successful organisations are given in Chapter 10 — History.

The reader may ask how it is that no one in the West appears to know about such an important development in Eastern Europe. The main answer is that "nobody wants to know". This may seem surprising: but it is the normal human reaction to any idea of really fundamental change. We are prepared

1

for some modification of the established concepts of our lives: but, if it is proposed to abandon any of them entirely and do something quite different, our minds rebel. We may think that we are considering such an idea impartially: but, all the time, a little man at the back of our minds is saying "by all means amuse yourself with this, but of course you know its quite impossible". Consequently, whatever our conscious reasoning may tell us about the idea of worker-ownership, subconsciously we have no intention of accepting it.

Sub-consciously therefore we seek reasons for rejecting the evidence of Mondragon and for refraining from any enquiries into Eastern Europe. We thus find that we can set Mondragon aside as suitable only for Basques, and that we can dismiss evidence from behind the Iron Curtain as sure to be phony. This enables us to go on ascribing our industrial troubles to incompetent management or intransigent trade unions, and to avoid the uncomfortable possibility of having to consider changing the basis of our whole industrial system. Economists in particular are spared the danger of having to discard most of their existing expertise and to start learning economics afresh.

In fact it is really quite easy to go (for example) to Budapest, where enquiry will discover that the whole small business sector of the Hungarian economy is operated by worker-owned businesses, and that such businesses produce 70% of Hungarian agricultural output. Further enquiry will show that these demonstrations of industrial democracy are perfectly genuine, even if they are politically limited in extent. It will then appear — and this is the important point — that the enterprises in Hungary are organised in a remarkably similar manner to those in Spain: and wider enquiry will disclose the same general pattern in Poland, Czechoslovakia and Romania.

B — Industrial Democracy

"Neither fish, flesh, fowl nor good red herring" — Trad.

The reader will object that, whatever may have happened elsewhere, the record of workers co-operatives in most Western countries has been one of failure. However this is because the practice of industrial democracy contains pitfalls, especially for those with an aversion to making any fundamental change. In the practice of political democracy, we have learned the importance of maintaining certain principles like secret voting and freedom of information. We know how easy it is to create a facade of political democracy, without having its reality. Exactly the same danger arises with industrial democracy. If it is to have reality, it too requires the maintenance of certain principles.

Unfortunately (for reasons which are explained in Chapter 9 — Definition) the workers co-operative movement never evolved any principles of its own. As a result its operation of industrial democracy was adulterated in two ways. Firstly, enterprises were often created without a complete change-over from capital ownership to worker-ownership. Secondly, further ethical and social aims were often grafted onto the simple idea of control of work by people at work. Cooperatives thus often failed to conform to, or to limit themselves to, the essential principles of industrial democracy. Consequently, even where individual co-operatives have been a commercial success, they have failed to demonstrate that new world of freedom which genuine industrial democracy opens up. By contrast, the success of the Mondragon and East European movements (as explained in Chapter 10) resulted from their logical adherence to the idea of complete and unadulterated worker-ownership.

It might be thought that industrial democracy could evolve in the same way as has political democracy, through a gradual increase in the power of the people. However this is hardly possible. Political democracy has only advanced when societies have been free from war — and hence its increase in those parts of the world where foreign conquest is now out of fashion. But this is just what is denied to business enterprises competing with each other in a conventional Western economy. If a business is to survive in the battle of commerce, either it must retain the advantages of dictatorship by conventional capital ownership, or it must acquire the full motivating effect of democracy by means of complete worker-ownership. Half-and-half arrangements can only hope to succeed where enterprises consist of rather unusual people, willing to forego the normal aims of ordinary workers.

C — The Need for Theory

"He who will not reason is a bigot; he who cannot is a fool; and he who dare not is a slave" — William Drummond

Many people would like to see 'the workers' having some share in the profits and the control of the businesses in which they work. Hence such ideas as ESOPS and 'quality circles'. Measures of this nature may indeed improve the functioning of the conventional capital ownership system. However it is not practical to convert a business to worker-ownership by such means. Once the workers in a business acquire any substantial degree of its control and its profits, the capitalists will withdraw.* Even the state requires control of the enterprises which it finances.

*Unless they are people deliberately arranging for their business to be taken over by its workers.

3

This brings us up against the problem that worker-owners have to borrow any capital which they cannot provide themselves and that, in order to do this, they have to give it security. At this point, the little man in the reader's sub-conscious mind says "Oh nonsense! Everyone knows that risk capital is essential to industry". All the same, the operation of businesses with risk labour in place of risk capital* can be seen in practice in both Mondragon and Eastern Europe. The way in which it works is explained in Chapter 11 — Finance.

It follows that people who wish to investigate worker-ownership must first acquire some knowledge of its theory. They must start by deciding whether it is really worker-ownership which they wish to examine, or whether they seek no more than some form of 'participation' within the conventional capital ownership system. Then, if industrial democracy is indeed their aim, they must decide what are its essential conditions. In other words they have to define a worker-owned business. Clearly it is no good an enquirer going and looking at co-operatives without knowing what does, and what does not, constitute genuine industrial democracy. The matter is examined in detail in Chapter 9 — Definition.

An enquirer has also to consider whether an apparently successful worker-owned business is demonstrating something which will attract other workers to go and do likewise. An unusually able manager may bring commercial success to almost any kind of business. What the enquirer has to look for is a number of businesses which operate genuine worker-ownership, which do it in the same way, which are mostly successful, and which have a waiting list of new members.

D — Semantics

"You see it's like a portmanteau: there are two meanings packed up in the one word" — Lewis Carroll

The meanings of various terms and phrases generally used in connection with the subject matter of this book are explained, as follows:-

Worker-ownership is the term used in this book to describe a system in which business enterprises are owned and controlled by the people who supply them with labour, instead of by the people who supply them with capital. Such enterprises are commonly known as co-operatives: but that word carries with it certain further ideas which are not a necessary part of worker-ownership.

Employee Ownership is an alternative term to the above: but it is not used in this book because joint business owners, whatever their technical position

---

*Meaning capital (private or public) supplied at risk in the hope of profit.

4

under the law, are not employees in any factual sense. Employment for wages and salaries is in fact the system from which they have escaped.

Co-operatives can take various forms, but the two main types are 'consumer' and 'producer'. A consumer co-operative is an enterprise controlled by its customers by means of capital ownership: whilst a producer co-operative is an enterprise controlled by its workers by means of worker-ownership.

Ownership & Control are two sides of the same coin, because control is the meaning and purpose of ownership. It should not be necessary to use the phrase 'ownership and control' because the one word connotes the other. Unfortunately the law sometimes divides their meaning, as when a tenant is given rights over a property owned by a landlord. The true position in such a case is that some of the natural rights of ownership are taken from the landlord and given to the tenant.

Capitalism & Socialism are imprecise terms, which can be interpreted differently by different people. This book is not concerned with the 'capitalist system' (whatever that may mean) but with a change-over from capital control of work to labour control of work.

Capitalists & Workers may easily be the same people. In this book a capitalist is assumed to be a person whose concern with a business is the supply of money to it, whilst a worker is a person who supplies it with labour.

Wages & Profits are words, the normal meaning of which alters in conditions of worker-ownership. The word 'wages' becomes meaningless, whilst the word 'profits' signifies the residual income of a business before, instead of after, the remuneration of the workers. This is further explained in Appendix K.

Private & Public ownership are two different forms of conventional capital control of work. Worker-ownership is the opposite of both of them: and it is misleading to describe it as a 'third system' or a 'middle way'.

Free Enterprise is generally taken to mean private capital ownership operating in a market economy. However worker-ownership is equally private and equally able to operate in a market economy. It is in fact the most free form of free enterprise.

Workers' Control ought properly to mean the same thing as worker-ownership: but it is commonly used to imply a sharing of control by capital and labour, in which the workers exercise the control and the capitalists pay the wages.

Participation is a term used to indicate a share in the profits and control of a business by its workers, but with the capitalist owners in ultimate control.

Self-Management is a term coined by the Yugoslavs to describe their system, in which the rights of ownership are divided between the workers in a business and the local authority.

5

Common Ownership is a term used in Britain to denote worker-owned businesses belonging to a particular organisation, in which the capital of a business is usually held collectively. The term is also applied to worker-owned businesses generally in N.S.W., Australia.

Workplace Democracy is the term used by an organisation which promotes worker-ownership in the U.S.A.

Men & Women belong to the same species. Some species have a generic name, whilst others are known by one of their genders. Thus deer describes either stags or hinds, but ducks is how we speak of both ducks and drakes. In the case of humans we can use either method: so that we can equally well say that "men cannot fly" or that "people cannot fly". However the latter practice can be inconvenient in writing a book. It is much easier to write that "if you praise a man he will do his work better" than that "if you praise a person he or she will do his or her work better".

The former practice has therefore been adopted here. A 'chairman' thus signifies a male or female person taking the chair at a meeting — and a 'man-eating tiger' means either a tiger or a tigress which will (if it gets the chance) eat either a man or a woman.

PART I — THEORY

"A Capitalist"

1 — Capital Control

"Let us ask what is best, not what is customary" — Seneca

Synopsis

A Visitor from outer space would find our control of work odd.

Human History shows how this system arose.

Village Industry was satisfactory under this system in the past.

Trade Unions became necessary in the factory age.

Resistance to Change was demonstrated then, as now.

Limited Liability accentuated the changes of the industrial revolution.

Managerial Control of business enterprises is an illusion.

State Control of industry is just another form of capital control.

The Capitalists are practically all of us.

The Solution is to give people control of their own work.

A Visitor

Will the reader imagine that he gets up one morning to find a flying saucer parked outside the front door. From this apparatus there emerges a polite gentleman, who explains that he is a visitor from outer space studying the arrangements on earth. He is particularly interested in the way in which we humans produce goods and services for each other. He says that he understands how the average business operates, with collections of people working under the direction of managers: but he has one query. Who is in ultimate control of such undertakings? Who sets them up and appoints the managers?

You reply that ultimate control rests with the people who provide the means of production (buildings, machinery etc) which the workers and their managers use. "Who are these people?", says the gentleman. You explain that they are either private shareholders, who join in subscribing the necessary. risk capital, or they are the citizens in general, who subscribe the money by paying taxes to their government. "How is it", says the gentleman, "that these shareholders (or citizens in general) know more about a business than the people actually working in it?" You explain that of course this is not so. These people only exercise ultimate control in order to protect their risk capital. Everything is in fact decided by the managers in the business.

9

"Yes, I see", says the gentleman, "but I don't understand why it is necessary for these providers of capital to take the risks. Why don't the workers appoint their own managers, borrow the necessary capital and take the risks themselves?" You answer that no such arrangement could be made to work. "Oh come now", says the gentleman, "are you telling me that such an arrangement is really beyond the wit of human beings?". "Well", you say, "I daresay it could be done: but the results would be thoroughly unsatisfactory." "How do you know that?", says the gentleman. "Because", you reply, "control of industry by the suppliers of the means of production has been the custom all over the Earth since the dawn of history." "Surely", you add, "that is evidence enough?" "Well", says the gentleman, "it is evidence that you operate your present method of controlling industry because that is how you have always done it in the past."

With these words, your visitor climbs back into his machine and disappears into the sky. You are left wondering whether it is necessarily correct to do something in a given way, just because that is how it has always been done in the past.

Human History

Men first appeared on earth as hunters and gatherers. Different families and tribes soon established rights to particular areas, in which they controlled the hunting and gathering. When men took to agriculture, control of work became even more firmly vested in the owners of the land which was 'the means of production'. It might have been better if men had continued the old hunting custom of joint action under a village leader, with the rewards shared by all. However villages and tribes soon started fighting with each other for land. This gave rise to conquerors and kings who acquired the ownership of land, and who often created slaves and serfs to work it for them. A free man was one who could claim a wage for cultivating another man's land, in place of having to work for nothing.

When men produced goods and services, they adopted the same arrangement of giving control of work to those who provided the means of production. It was natural to accept the inventor of a tool or process as the best leader of the work which made use of that tool or process. It was also natural for the abler men who thus initiated production to take for themselves both the risks and the rewards of their ventures. Hired labour thus became the rule in industry as in agriculture.

Further, this universal custom of control of work by the providers of the means of production was generally quite satisfactory in the days of village industry. No doubt a system of industrial democracy would have been theoretically better: but, in those days, it would have made little practical difference.

10

Village Industry

Until not so very long ago, goods and services were all produced by "the butcher, the baker, the candlestick maker", with the cobbler, carpenter, mason, blacksmith, wheelwright etc, in the local village or small town. In those days a 'manufacturer' was a man who made things and a 'shop' the place where he both produced and sold them. Most of these manufacturers worked on their own or with one or perhaps two others. Half a dozen men working together was a big village enterprise.

In such conditions of industry master and men worked side by side on the same bench or in the same shop, and every worker could express his opinions and be sure of having his views taken into account. When three men made shoes in a cobbler's shop, they all knew what the leather and thread cost and what the customers paid, and they could all see how much each contributed to the business. Wages were primarily a means of dividing up their joint earnings. If the amount taken by the employer exceeded the value of his own labour, this was only acceptable to the extent that his direction or his shop equipment increased the earnings of the business. His authority normally stemmed, not so much from ownership, as from his position as the senior workman. If he died and his son took over, and if that son failed to pay due deference to the then senior workman, that man probably went off with his tools and set up on his own.

Of course differences of opinion arose between people at work, as they do now. There were mean employers and idle workers: but, in any disagreements, the powers of capital and labour were fairly evenly matched. When (as was quite common) the work force of a business comprised the owner and one man, a threat by that man to quit was as potent as a threat by his employer to sack him. The result was that they had to get along with each other.

We can still observe this situation in small farming communities. It is unwise for either a farm owner or a farm worker to 'get himself a bad name'. If a farmer changes his worker(s) too often, the next time he wants a worker nobody applies for the job. Equally a farm worker who keeps changing his job soon finds that no one offers him one. In such communities we may hear a farmer complaining that he cannot get old George to plough a field in a certain way: but, if old George is generally a good man (and probably a respected member of the community), the farmer would never think of forcing the issue. Similarly, young Bob may have a hangover one morning and give the farmer a back answer: but, if young Bob is normally a good worker, the farmer will turn a deaf ear. In return, George and Bob will work all hours to get the harvest in.

Trade Unions

A great change came about with the industrial revolution, which began a process of dis-associating masters and men. The people who had previously

11

made things in villages, either on their own or as small employers or as valued workmen, now found themselves all employed in the local factory. The employer was no longer a fellow workman, but a 'director' in an office. Arrangements could no longer be discussed naturally and informally by master and men at work. Indeed the processes of production got beyond the vision of the man on the bench. Even the employer had to use complicated costing methods in order to discover whose work produced what results. The old atmosphere of joint endeavour for shared rewards disappeared.

This changed situation between masters and men soon gave rise to frictions which had never existed before. At the same time the ordinary man, instead of being an essential part of some village business, found himself one of (perhaps) a hundred 'hands' in the local factory. He could leave his job, or be dismissed, without his absence causing anyone more than minor inconvenience. He was thus at the mercy of his employer, on whose moods and whims his own livelihood might depend. The new factories had destroyed the old equilibrium between capital and labour. It is obvious now how the balance of power needed to be restored by collective bargaining.

Resistance to Change

However what seems simple and obvious to us now was not in the least so to people at the time. In the days of village industry, it had been the custom for each man to make his own employment bargain. There were circumstances in which employers managed to control wage levels, to the detriment of workers: but these were unusual. Attempts to form a 'ring', by either employers or employees, were regarded as anti-social. The new factory owners thus felt righteously indignant at demands for collective bargaining, which were indeed viewed with doubt by the workers themselves. The major problem for the new trade union organisers was that of inculcating the idea of 'solidarity of the workers'. They were regarded as extremists, not only by their employers, but often by their fellow workers too.

We tend to look back now with a feeling of superiority at the stupidity of both employers and workers, who took so long to see the effect of the changes which had taken place around them. We look at pictures of funny old directors in wing collars and of workmen in bowler hats: and it never occurs to us that they were all people remarkably like ourselves. In particular, the employers (who created the immense changes of the industrial revolution) were just the same kind of alert and progressive men as those who run great industrial corporations today. If therefore those people failed to notice fundamental changes in their environment, what reason is there to suppose that we, their descendants, will do any better?

That is of course the theme of this book. We now fail to discern the changes in our industrial environment, which make our continued operation of capital control of work an anachronism. Unfortunately 'what we learn from history is that we do not learn from history'.

Limited Liability

It will be apparent that, had worker-ownership been the system when the industrial revolution took place, no problems would have arisen. People would simply have continued democratic control of their own work in larger units. However if most of them at first failed to see the need for collective bargaining, they were hardly likely to see the need for industrial democracy.* Consequently, when a further change in the industrial scene took place, which further reduced cooperation between employers and employees, its effect was simply to hasten the rise of the trade unions.

If masters and men were separated by the conditions of the factory age, they were further distanced by the changes which followed the British Limited Liability Act of 1863. During the ensuing hundred years the capitalist owners of industry gradually left the factories they had created: so that, by the second half of the twentieth century, most of them took no part at all in the enterprises which they owned. The controllers of people at work today are either faceless shareholders of privately owned industry, or nameless electors in ultimate control of state enterprises. We may understand how this situation came about: but it is surprising that we allow such an absurd arrangement to continue. However people have had their attention diverted by two things.

The first diversion (as already noted) was the evolution of trade unions, which redressed the balance of power in industry. These were so obviously beneficial that people tended to see in them the answer to all the problems of capital and labour. However they are a palliative rather than a cure. They enable opposing parties to get along together: but they tend to accentuate, rather than to alleviate, the fact of opposition. They clearly fail to create a happy community of interest between capital and labour.

The second diversion was provided by Karl Marx. Despite what has been written above, there were some people who queried the whole system. One of these was Marx: but unfortunately, although he saw the problem, he just missed the solution. In 1866 Marx worded a resolution of The Provisional General Council of the International Working Mens Association, which read as follows:- "We recommend to the working man to embark on co-operative production rather than co-operative stores. The latter touch but the surface of the economic system, the former attacks its groundwork." Had Marx and his followers not been side-tracked by the idea of a class war, the world might by now have been a very different place.

*We now realise how very far sighted were people like Robert Owen and John Mill.

13

Managerial Control

The defence of the present system of capital control of work is that its practical result is the control of business enterprises by skilled management. However this is an illusion. Industry is controlled by its capitalists owners, because it is they who decide its objective. We mostly fail to appreciate this, because the objective of the suppliers of capital is so simple. All they want is the best return on their money, by way of interest and(or capital appreciation. For practical purposes this means the highest production at the lowest cost.* Provided managers stick to this objective, the owners of industry are happy to let them make all the detailed arrangements. Further, a system has been evolved which compels managers to make this their objective without obvious action by the owners of industry. The system is the stock market, and its watch dog is the take-over bidder.

The ordinary shareholder expresses his opinion of different teams of business managers when he buys and sells his shares on the stock market. Share prices thus become the gauge of managerial success or failure. Although most shareholders would deny having any power over the managers who run their businesses, the system in fact gives them powers which they exercise with devastating effect if occasion arises. All they have to do is to accept a take-over bid. What the take-over bidder does (in effect) is to say to the shareholders of a business — "Your managers are not making as much money for you as they could, in proof of which I will offer you a much higher price for your shares than the present stock market figure". The shareholders happily accept the resultant capital gain, mostly without realising that what they have done is to dismiss their managers. However the managers of their business know all right: and the lesson is not lost on management in general.

In the past, some managerial teams made a practice of 'writing down' the assets of their business in times of prosperity, so as to have a concealed reserve. This was because managers, like all workers, want security more than the maximum possible earnings. It was precisely this practice which produced the take-over bidder, who saw that what most shareholders want is maximum appreciation of their shares on comparatively short term. Since the appearance of the take-over bidder, that managerial practice has ceased!

So effective is capital control of industry that industrial managers automatically assume their objective to be the highest production.* Indeed nearly everyone assumes this. Few people realise, firstly that 'production' is not the only possible object of people at work, and secondly that it is capital ownership of industry which imposes this object on all concerned.

---

*The phrase 'highest production' is used here to mean the production and sale of whatever goods and/or services will provide the enterprise with the highest net financial return in the reasonably near future, i.e. within a period which will be much less than the working lives of its employees.

14

State Control

The fact that there was (and is) something wrong with the way industry works has been evidenced by the demand for state ownership. Reformers thought that it was 'private profit' which caused people's dissatisfaction. They assumed that, if the benevolent state could replace the 'wicked' private capitalist, all would be well. They failed to see that it was not the source of capital which was wrong, but the fact of capital control itself.

The trouble with state ownership is that the legislators have to please the voters. Although few voters expect profits from state industry, they do wish to avoid losses. They also dislike paying a lot for the goods or services produced by state enterprises. At the same time they know nothing at all about the different enterprises they control. In fact, as the capitalist owners of industry, voters are in much the same position as ordinary shareholders.

The people's representatives are aware of this. Consequently they give to state managers the same objective as that given by private shareholders to their managers, which is the most production at the lowest cost. They add an instruction "be nice to the workers": but that is also what private shareholders say to their managers. In both cases the managers are aware that what this means in practice is - "we don't mind what you do about the workers (because we will never know) so long as you avoid a strike". The subject is dealt with in greater detail at Appendix A.

The Capitalists

It is important to understand that nearly everyone is both a capitalist and a worker. Few people can afford not to work, and most of us supply industry with money one way or another. Admittedly the number of private shareholders is limited: but 'institutions' are now the main shareholders in industry. These institutional investors in industry comprise such undertakings as banks, insurance companies and pension funds. The picture of the capitalist owners of industry as paunchy individuals in top hats is misleading.

Let us take an example of what can actually happen. Let us imagine a keen trade unionist, who goes on a well-earned holiday with his family, and who prudently takes out a holiday insurance policy. The man naturally chooses the insurance company which will give him the best value for his money. Let us assume that, by chance, this insurance company happens to invest some of its funds in the very business in which the man works. What can happen as a result is that —

- the man says (in effect) to the insurance company manager, "Give me the best possible value for my money".
- the insurance company manager, when investing its money in the business

15

which employs the man, says (in effect) to the business manager, "Give us the best possible return on our money".

- the manager of that company then says (in fact) to the man, "Get a bloody move on with your work".
- the man then says (in fact) to the manager, "You horrible capitalist lackey, how dare you try to bully me."

As the reader can see, the situation of this man is initiated by his own actions. As a capitalist he starts the chain of oppression from which, as a worker, he suffers. This illustrates the point that, if we feel oppressed in the existing economic system of capital control of work, it is because the system is such as to induce us to oppress ourselves.

The Solution

The solution is to change from the conventional system of capital control of work to a system of worker control of work.

It should be noted that this has nothing to do with workers taking part in management. Managers are expert workers employed by business owners. The extent to which the business owners exercise detailed control of their management is for them to decide. In this connection most people at work require only two things. One is that ultimate control of their businesses shall be in their own hands. The other is that their managers shall be persons devoted to the benefit of themselves (the people at work).

It should also be noted that a system of worker-ownership means control of work exercised by people in their capacity as suppliers of labour to a business, instead of in their capacity as suppliers of capital to it.

Summary

It seems an odd idea that the people who work in a business should accept control of their enterprise by another lot of people who supply it with money. However this system arose naturally in the world and was quite satisfactory in the days of village industry.

Unfortunately the arrival of the factory age, coupled with limited liability, has so altered the circumstances of work that the conventional system of capital control is now quite irrational.

People fail to see this, partly because history shows us that changes in our environment are always difficult to discern, and partly because attention has been diverted by the rise of trade unions and the theories of Karl Marx.

It is an illusion to think that industry is controlled by management, because the capitalist owners of industry compel managers to make 'production' their objective.

We are nearly all capitalists, because nearly all of us supply industry with money, directly or indirectly. If therefore we are oppressed at work, it is mostly because we oppress ourselves.

The solution is to change our system of capital ownership of industry to one of worker-ownership.

"Divided Industry"

2 — The Divided Nation

"A house divided against itself shall fall" — St Luke's Gospel.

Synopsis

Change is needed to escape from slavery and to embrace opportunity.

Industrial Slavery is what we suffer.

Workers Needs are explained

Disunity is bad and results from failure to meet workers needs.

The English Disease is a symptom of this disunity .

Spread of the disease is explained.

The Remedy is industrial democracy.

Change

It is shown in the previous chapter that we operate a system of controlling work which was evolved in quite different conditions from those now existing, and which has thus become an anachronism. However if this system does in fact 'produce the goods', then why worry? What is the need for change?

The answer is twofold —

- Firstly, there is an enormous gain to be made by giving people freedom at work. In Appendix B is an extract from a speech given to the United Nations, which claims that the democratic West needs some great new idea which will counter the communist ideal. Genuine industrial democracy can be just that.
- Secondly, the developed nations need to escape from the division of their peoples into two predictable parties of Capital and Labour. Disunity is a deadly disease, which we must overcome.

Industrial Slavery

Whilst it is an exaggeration to picture workers in industry as 'slaves', and whilst many people lead perfectly happy lives at work, there is another side to the picture shown by the following —

- In Britain in 1924, the Labour Party and the Trades Union Congress produced a document entitled The Waste of Capitalism, an extract from which is given in Appendix C. More than half a century later many of the emotive words in that document still ring true: and its statement that "there is likely to be more and more friction and less and less production if a remedy is not found" has proved an accurate forecast of British industry.

19

- When the 'Sankey Commission' took evidence on the state of the British coal mining industry, a miner's official William Straker said:
  "Industrial unrest is a question about which everyone is concerned, yet there is a general lack of appreciation of what is the real root of the unrest. In the past, workmen have thought that, if they could secure higher wages and better conditions, they would be content. Employers thought that if they granted these things the workers ought to be content. Wages and conditions have improved, but the discontent and unrest have not disappeared. The fact is that discontent is deeper than can be reached by mere pounds, shillings and pence, necessary as they are. The root of the matter is the straining of the spirit of man to be free."
- A recent British trade union leader, Hugh Scanlon, said: "Political democracy is no longer viable in a structure possessing an undemocratic industrial system. It is arrant nonsense to talk about the development of democracy without at the same time putting industrial democracy at the forefront. Undoubtedly the final role of the trade unions will be to change society itself, instead of getting the best out of existing society."
- At an earlier date, the same idea of escaping from the system of employment was put forward by trade union officials in America. William Sylvis, the president of an early American trade union, said: "The cause of all these evils is the wages system. So long as we continue to work for wages, so long will we continue to be subject to the evils of which we complain." T.V. Powderly, another member, said: "The aim of our union, properly understood, is to make each man his own master. It is intended by the Knights of Labour to supersede the wages system by a system of cooperation." Another member, A.M. Wright, said: "We do not believe that the emancipation will come with increased wages and a reduction in the hours of work: we must go deeper than that, and this matter will not be settled until the wages system is abolished."
- Some lines in a novel about a French village conjure up a delightful picture of freedom at work — "Every Summer the Italian chair makers would arrive. They would select a cherry tree growing in somebody's orchard, chop it down, saw it up with swift beautiful precision and, in three days time, there they would stand — one's new chairs, ready for use and far better than any chairs one could buy in the neighbouring town." Alas, modern methods of manufacture 'in the neighbouring town' have since overtaken those Italian chair makers: but who can doubt their fulfilment as they worked together 'with swift beautiful precision'.

Workers' Needs

In the days of village industry, when men normally worked and lived in the same place, local democratic institutions like the Parish Council provided a forum for industrial as well as for social problems. Political democracy was required only to free people from tyrannical actions by a distant national government. Unfortunately, the passing of the Great Reform Bill in the 19th century signalled the final achievement of political democracy in Britain, just when the factory age had created an urgent need for industrial democracy.

This is not to say that ordinary people did (or do) want to manage their businesses. The ordinary man at work wants to get on with his own job, leaving management to the managers. However he does have two requirements. Firstly, he wants to be able (in company with his mates) to control the conditions of his job, free from tyrannical decisions from above. He understands the need for work to be integrated by management: but he wants to have the ultimate power to refuse to work in ways he really dislikes. Secondly, he wants his work to be managed by people who are 'on his side'. He has a basic human desire to be part of a team pursuing joint objectives. This is rarely possible in circumstances in which management's first loyalty is to capitalist business owners.

It is these two basic requirements which cause workers to support trade unions. It is only unions which have the power to oppose management, and it is only union officials whose prime concern is with the workers. That is why, in the event of a dispute, the workers always back their union. They may not have a high opinion of their union officials, and they may regard their managers as reasonable and intelligent men: but, in a capital ownership system, the managers are unavoidably 'on the other side'.

This situation places much power in the hands of union officials because, as noted above, the average worker wants to get on with his own job. That was brought out some years ago by an interview with a shop steward in Ford Motors of Britain. Bernie Passingham said: "What the shop stewards may decide, he (the ordinary worker) would tend to accept, because that's the normal practice of a lad on the shop floor. He puts his trust and faith, believe it or not, in his shop steward. You might not believe it when you read the papers, but that basically is it."

Unfortunately this power is not wholly beneficial. For example trade unions are liable to impose additional controls on working men, such as the 'closed shop'. They also tend to emphasise the 'war' between the two sides of industry. The author once attended a Left wing trade union conference, which was addressed (in excellent English) by a union official from Italy. The Italian explained, with some pride, exactly how his members had succeeded in reducing the output of the Fiat Motor Co by no less than 140,000 units. He never said, nor did any of his audience ask, how this benefited the Fiat workers. It was enough, apparently, to have damaged the 'wicked capitalists'.

Disunity

Men owe their supremacy over the animal world to their greater brains, which give them the ability to work together. A man alone in the jungle is a

21

feeble creature, at the mercy of his environment: but communities of men working together can nowadays literally 'move mountains'. Any division of a human society thus strikes at the roots of its success. This is the great problem of the Western world. People in modern societies feel themselves divided into the rich and the poor, the 'haves' and the 'have-nots', the Left and the Right. This outlook colours discussion of every national problem. Different citizens should hold many different views on such complex problems as communications, defence, health, education etc: but national policies are mostly judged, not on their merits, but on the advantages they will bring respectively to Left or to Right.

We tend to be prisoners of our environment. In each epoch we take certain assumptions for granted, without realising that some of them are peculiar to our particular time. For example it was assumed in the past that religion automatically divided people. It would then have seemed absurd to suggest that there need be no antagonism between Protestants and Catholics. Similarly today we take for granted the divisive effect of there being rich and poor in society. We assume that poor people must naturally feel an antagonism for those who are better off. What we fail to realise is that this attitude is a comparatively recent phenomenon. It appears to be natural and obvious now: but as short a time as 200 years ago it hardly existed.

Of course people disagreed in the past, even resorting to arms: but their antagonisms were normally on national or geographical or religious grounds. Rich and poor together on one side fought rich and poor together on the other side. The argument that the poor were compelled to fight by the rich is believable only by those who have never taken part in battle. Soldiers pressed to fight unwillingly soon manage to run away.

People have always accepted their inequality. It is inevitable that some men are born handsomer or cleverer or more athletic than others: and these lucky individuals will inevitably acquire more of this world's advantages, whether directly in the form of money or indirectly through power and influence. Of course poorer persons have always envied those who were richer (as the weak have always envied the strong): but, prior to the industrial revolution, there were grades of poverty and riches (as there are still grades of physical skill). It was not possible for half the citizens (the 'workers') to identify themselves as naturally separated from the other half of the citizens.

The modern idea that we cannot get along together whilst there are inequalities of wealth between us is equivalent to saying that we all require to be born with the same amount of talent. If we deny extra money to the abler members of society, they merely find other ways of benefiting themselves — as we see in the supposedly egalitarian countries of Eastern Europe. If equality is the aim, how do we prevent the very pretty girl from enjoying advantages denied to her plainer sisters? In fact it is not possible to combine both equality and freedom. As Robert Ardrey has written — "Injustice is opportunity suppressed, not just by the totalitarian, but by the egalitarian as well".

The real cause of our disunity lies in industry. The poorer half of the citizens, 'the workers', feel themselves controlled and exploited by their employers. This feeling of antagonism in industry colours their view of all social problems. The workers condemn people richer than themselves because they equate them with the capitalist employers, whom they have come to regard as their natural enemies. They did not have this feeling in the days of village industry, when disparities of wealth were much greater than they are now. It arose only in the factory age. As the historian G.M. Trevelyan has written — "There was less communication, it was remarked, between the mill hand and his master than between a duke and the humblest worker on his estate". Trevelyan added that "it was a sign of the social schism which was to grow into a yawning gap in the next half century". That gap still yawns: and it is widest in the 'dark satanic mills' of large scale production, where people are farthest from the old conditions of village industry. The gap will be closed, not by abolishing millionaires or dukes, but by giving people control of their own work.

Further examples of the feelings of 'them' and 'us' in industry are given in Appendix D — Disunity at Work.

The English Disease

History shows that successful societies have always been united ones. The Romans had no great leader like Hannibal of Carthage: but they had confidence in each other as Roman citizens. The explorers and traders, who went out to the new world from Spain, regarded themselves as exponents of a superior culture. The British Victorians, who initiated the industrial revolution, were the inhabitants of a tight little island which had defeated Napoleon. It was belief in themselves which made Japanese soldiers the bravest in the second world war. By contrast, it was national disunity which caused the fall of France in 1940.

There is something pathetic about the memorials of the first world war to be seen in every village in Britain. This is not because men died, but because they died in defence of a society which so many of their descendants now condemn. It is difficult to recapture the flavour of 1914, when men volunteered to fight for no better reason than that Britain was their country. Although the seeds of disunity had already germinated in the factories of the industrial revolution, they had not then spread throughout the nation. Few people then pictured their society as it was portrayed only ten years later in the document given at Appendix C.

The upheavals of two world wars accelerated the changes in outlook, which now result in so many British citizens being predictably divided between Left and Right. After each of these wars it was a common complaint that people

23

who had fought shoulder to shoulder in war found themselves opposed to each other in peace. Some blamed the employers and their managers, whilst others blamed the workers and their unions. No one then saw that the trouble was due to an industrial system which naturally divides people at work into two sides, management and men.

It is no surprise that this disunity has been worst in Britain, because it is Britons who have had the longest experience both of the industrial revolution and (with Americans) of democratic practice. It is thus British workers who have reacted most strongly against the enslaving effects of work in the factory age. Unfortunately, few of their leaders have seen — as did William Straker — that 'the root of the matter is the straining of the spirit of man to be free'. British workers have thus been foremost in their demands for the more obvious benefits of higher pay and less work. This is what is called the English Disease. It arises, not because British workers are naturally idler and more grasping than others, but because they are the people least satisfied with the conditions brought about by the industrial revolution.

Comparison may be made with a Chinese waiter in a small restaurant in a village in the New Territories of Hongkong. He was no 'uneducated peasant'. He spoke English, as well as reading and writing Cantonese. He explained that he worked 13 hours a day for seven days a week, with a total of five days holiday a year. He turned down the suggestion of doing half the work for double the pay in England, on the grounds of climate. He appreciated having a job in a community subjected to vast inflows of people without jobs. He had no experience of democracy. He was living in a 'village industry' community. His conditions of work would have caused a British trade union official to have an apoplectic fit: but the man was not in fact unduly discontented with his lot.

The breeding ground of the English Disease is experience of the conditions of the factory age, a democratic tradition and a degree of affluence.

Spread

Since some other developed countries suffer less from the English Disease, it may be thought that its incidence can be confined. However both democracy and industrialisation are spreading: and, whilst they are combined with the capital ownership system, disunity is bound to result. Special circumstances have so far limited the disease in (for example) Germany and America.

The Germans had a history of success resulting from following their leaders in war, rather than from democracy. Then they suffered the trauma of defeat and occupation in the second world war. People faced with starvation do not argue with employers who provide them with the means of survival. However memories of the past are fading: so that even in West Germany there is now some division between Left and Right.

Americans might claim a longer experience of democracy than Britons: but this did not apply to the waves of penniless immigrants who were thankful for any kind of work in the new world. America was also the 'land of opportunity', where anyone who objected to the conditions of his work could 'go West, young man'. Until recently therefore, Americans were not constrained in the same way as most Europeans to accept particular conditions of work which they disliked. That is why it is only recently that the two great political parties in America have become identified with Left and Right.

It is only Japan which appears to be immune. The special circumstances which account for this, and which cannot be exported, are explained in Appendix E.

The Remedy

The remedy for autocracy is democracy. If therefore we are divided because of disunity in industry, the answer is to unify industry by means of worker-ownership. Then management and men can work happily together: and industrial democracy can offer people the kind of 'hope for the masses' envisaged by C.H. Malik in Appendix B.

It may be objected that, so far from unifying society, the remedy here proposed will merely be a triumph for the Left. It is thus important to understand that, although worker-ownership unifies industry by removing the capitalist 'side', this will not damage capitalists, i.e. people who invest money in industry (as explained in detail under 'Capital Reward' in Chapter 6.) This point was made as long ago as 1913 by a certain Father Finlay. Speaking to a producer co-operative meeting in Ireland, he said — "Our movement makes no war on capital or capitalist. We aim at being capitalists ourselves, at amassing for the group which works co-operatively the necessary funds for the operations carried on for the common benefit. But with us the individual and the society obtain capital by work and not by plunder. In doing so we concede the same right to everyone else who chooses to enter the field of industry in which we are occupied. The idea of a war of classes is wholly alien to our movement which, by its nature, makes for social and economic peace."

It may also be objected that, if capitalists can no longer be the enemy, the workers will merely fight amongst themselves — as we see in trade union disputes. However the point is, not that people will cease to disagree with one another, but that the industrial system will no longer encourage disagreement. You do not stop people from killing each other by abolishing war: but you make killing a social crime instead of a patriotic duty.

Finally it may be objected that worker-ownership is being put forward as a kind of 'universal panacea' for all the ills of society. To an appreciable extent this is just what the author is doing. The scientific 'principle of parsimony'

25

(otherwise known as Ockham's Razor) holds that the simplest explanation of diverse phenomena is the one most likely to be right. The simple explanation of many of the diverse ills of present day society is that, whilst we have achieved political democracy, we lack industrial democracy.

Summary

People are liable to feel enslaved in industry. What they want is ultimate control of their own work, with their own leaders. Lacking this, they see industry as divided between the capitalists and their managers on one side and the workers and their trade unions on the other side.

This feeling spills over into society as a whole, so that the poor feel themselves naturally opposed to the rich. That attitude seems natural and obvious to us today: but in fact it never existed before the industrial revolution created two sides in industry. The disunity which it produces is very bad for human societies.

The English Disease, which appears to demonstrate idleness and greed, in fact demonstrates dissatisfaction with a lack of industrial democracy in the conditions of the factory age. The disease is spreading in all the developed countries, except Japan.

The remedy for national disunity is industrial democracy, made available by worker-ownership.

"The Object of Work"

3 — The Object of Work

"Work is a primary human need and method of self expression" — Martin Leighton

Synopsis

Affluence changes people's objectives in work.

Fulfilment of the worker is the object of work.

Capital Control makes workers fulfilment impossible.

Unpleasant Work is unnecessary.

Business Societies of human beings are what is needed.

The Difficulty is to enable people to find out what balance of satisfactions will best fulfil them at work.

The State has no duty to interfere.

Affluence

It has been shown how the industrial revolution changed the conditions of work so as to make people into 'wage slaves'. It initiated another change, which is the advent of affluence.

In the past people often used up all their energy in getting food, clothing and shelter. In such circumstances money is the overriding object of work. The poor emigrant, when he first lands on a foreign shore, will do any work in order to get a livelihood for his family. Once established however, he starts seeking some means of earning his bread without working quite so hard or in such unpleasant ways: and, as he progresses in the foreign land, so he is able to find better conditions of working. Eventually he achieves a position in which his children are able to pick and choose the way in which they will earn a living.

The improved position of people in developed countries has only become significant since the second world war. Prior to that, although legislation in most countries did greatly alleviate the conditions of work, this was seen as limiting what employers could demand rather than as providing people with satisfying conditions of work. It is really only in the second half of the twentieth century that ordinary people feel able to balance their wages against the other satisfactions offered by different forms of employment.

This is something which has always been available to the children of 'the rich', whose choice of profession automatically takes account both of the money likely to be earned and of the kind of life likely to be led. Now however, although they may not always realise it, almost everyone seeks a balance between the highest possible earnings (on an oil rig?) and various other advantages in any particular job. They choose whatever combination seems most likely to fulfil their desires and, since people's desires differ, the most we can say about the object of work is that it is the fulfilment of the worker.

Fulfilment

Prior to the industrial revolution a livelihood was often hard to get, but work (mostly on the land) was generally conducive to feelings of meaningful achievement. Nowadays, whilst it is easier for people to obtain the fulfilment of getting enough money on which to live, it is often harder for them to feel fulfilled by the kind of work they do. The importance of the kind of work is exemplified by the following —

- The 1924 document quoted at Appendix C contends that work should enable a man "to use his own intelligence and judgement, his own craftsmanship and artistic feeling, his own methods and theories". The document adds that "the sane human being has the desire to create, to change the material things round him, to affect his environment in the way his own nature dictates".
- In the same period Aldous Huxley condemned modern industry as creating conditions in which "people are related to one another, not as personalities, but as embodiments of industrial functions". He contended that "subjected to this kind of life, individuals tend to feel lonely and insignificant", and that "their existence ceases to have point or meaning".
- In 1964 M.S.Myer summarised his conclusions of a six year study of motivation in American industry by saying that the really important factor in workers' lives was "meaningful achievement", which he defined as "a sense of achievement in a responsible job, which earns the individual recognition and success". He found that "whenever opportunities for meaningful achievement are denied, workers become sensitised to their environment and begin to find fault with peripheral factors — such as schedules, lighting, coffee breaks, titles, seniority rights, wages, fringe benefits and the like".
- Martin Leighton, a recent enquirer into British industry, writes — "It is assumed that people only work from necessity and that creative work is a gift only given to the privileged few. In fact, work is a primary human need and method of self-expression, far outweighing the importance of earnings, and most people's jobs never come close to stretching their creative abilities. It is assumed that a manager's job is supervision and control of employees, that he should create and enforce detailed routines, and that these routines should be simple, repetetive and easily learned. In reality leadership is about releasing untapped human resources: and this is most likely to happen if the individual worker's responsibilities are broadened as far as possible and his capabilities challenged".

- A report by the British P.E.P. organisation quoted an industrial manager as saying — "I think that most of these financial incentives are just utter nonsense. Of course finance affects people. It affects us all because we would all like to have more money. But undoubtedly, beyond a certain level of money, what makes these people tick is a feeling that they are creating something and that, if they were not here, they would be missed".
- Finally, Karl Marx wrote in 1844 — "In what does the alienation of labour consist? That the work is external to the worker..that he does not fulfil himself, has a feeling of misery not of well-being..feels himself at home only during leisure, whereas at work he is homeless".

The practical manager, who has to deal with workers in industry, may feel that the above quotations exaggerate the psychological aspect of work, and that what workers really want is high pay and good conditions. However this is the view which the miners' leader William Straker (see Chapter 2) found to be mistaken, when he said that "the root of the matter is the straining of the spirit of man to be free". Why do people become shop stewards and trade union organisers? It cannot be for the money. If pay and conditions are what matter most to people, how does one account for the manifest fulfilment which soldiers feel in winning a battle? The conditions are appalling, and the reward at most a medal. It is true that many people take a job simply because they need the money: but, inevitably, they become concerned with the circumstances of their work and the degree of satisfaction it gives them.

There is a difficulty in assessing the importance of money, because it can be used both as a means of acquiring goods and as a yardstick of success. An American enquirer into workers' motivation wrote that "dissatisfaction with pay was more important as an act of unfairness than as a loss of money".

It is extremely difficult to decide just what combination of money and 'meaningful achievement' will best fulfil different collections of people at work in different circumstances. Furthermore it is quite wrong for us to try. Burke wrote that "the chief inlet by which oppression enters this world is by one man pretending to determine the happiness of another". All we can, and all we should, do is to let the people concerned in each business decide for themselves.

Capital Control

When taking the chair at the first board meeting of a newly acquired business, a British director is recorded as saying "Gentlemen, the product we are going to make in this business is money". This brings out the point that people do not invest money in a business in order to provide fulfilment for its workers. They invest money in order to make money. That does not mean to say that intelligent managers fail to see the advantages of fulfilling workers lives: but the two objectives often clash. An example of failure to provide for workers' fulfilment is given by Martin Leighton — "A manager's career will

31

reach a peak shortly before retirement. There is no such career development for the average manual worker. His earnings will be at their peak shortly after he completes his apprenticeship, and will decline thereafter with his physical powers.'' This may be an exaggeration. There are large businesses in which arrangements are specifically made to enable workers to increase their skills. Nevertheless it is still perfectly possible for a man aged 40 to find himself doing the same job for the same pay as his son aged 20. This is (surely?) an appalling situation

The difficulty is that action to increase workers' skills in a conventional business is only justified to the extent that it will produce greater profits in the reasonably near future. The fact that people are more likely to feel fulfilled by being given progressively more complicated work is of no interest to shareholders. At the same time the atmosphere of suspicion makes it impractical for management to help the workers to help themselves. It is unthinkable for the manager of a conventional business to say to his work force, "I propose to give you all more interesting work, which will increase your skills, in return for which you will have to agree to a slight reduction in wages". As is quoted about another managerial initiative in Appendix D, "we tried to get the shop stewards interested, but they just didn't trust us".

Unpleasant Work

The conditions of the factory age have led most of us to regard work as something which is inherently unpleasant. We are aware that unusual kinds of people — such as sculptors, inventors, explorers — do work which can be enjoyed. We wish our own work was less wearisome and dull. We fail to realise that it can be just as wearisome and dull to keep chipping bits off a block of marble or to struggle with recalcitrant formulae or to trudge along hot stony paths. Sculptors, inventors and explorers find fulfilment in their work, not because it is always so pleasant, but because they pursue objectives (which may include that of money) which they find worthwhile. It is equally possible for people in industry to do this, provided they are free to arrange their own work.

It may seem surprising that trades unions, negotiating on behalf of their members, take so little account of this aspect of work. The union negotiators do not say "we require the following arrangements to give our members greater feelings of fulfilment in their work". They say instead "we require more pay, shorter hours, and the discontinuance of certain practices which our members dislike". This may seem short-sighted: but it is comprehensible. Since people in the past had to work very hard to get enough on which to live, money has been the traditional object of work. This was why people left the countryside for the higher wages offered by the factories of the industrial revolution. Further, when account is taken of the fact that money is the object of those who control industry, and hence of their managers, it is not surprising that production for money is accepted as the object of work by all

32

concerned. As Aldous Huxley wrote, "so stern have been the forces channeling our thoughts in the past that there is little to go on in the fertile valleys of our imagination".

Business Societies

As explained, in the days of village industry people lived and worked in the same place. The industrial revolution produced both new forms of work and new forms of transport, so that it became possible for people to live in one place and work in another. In the places were people lived, their social lives continued to evolve: but, because of the assumption that work was concerned only with production for money, the places where they worked were not regarded as having any social significance. Even today we do not think of a business enterprise as a society of sentient human beings. We think of a business simply as an arrangement which will provide us with the money required for our social life at home.

Of course people who meet every day for work are bound to have some social relationship: but this is regarded as purely incidental to the purpose of the business. It is true that, particularly in regard to executives in America, there are attempts to identify families with the business which provides their livelihood: but most people in most businesses assume that they assemble together simply in order to earn a living. The evolution of our societies has thus taken place on the basis of our home rather than our working lives. We plan our education, our towns, our health and almost everything else by means of a residential vote.

The reader will see what very large changes can (and will) take place in circumstances in which business enterprises are owned by the people who work in them. The owners of a business will then be members of a mutual benefit society fulfilling themselves at work. No doubt they will mostly seek that fulfilment by producing goods or services which earn them money: but, if they are successful, it would be perfectly reasonable for the members of a worker-owned business to decide to hire an aeroplane to take them all to Las Vegas for a week-end! If there had been a system of worker-ownership when people first migrated from the country, business enterprises would now be very different organisations. People would have spent the last 150 years evolving them as happy places, where the members could enjoy providing their fellow citizens with goods and services.*

* An elderly Japanese industrialist, Sazo Idemitsu, answered a question about the object of work as follows: "A salary is required to secure one's livelihood, but it is not the object of work itself. Now, if a salary is not the object of labour, one may ask where the object lies. My answer is that it is in the satisfaction which a man feels when he works free from restraint on the job best suited to himself and his abilities. A man can enjoy such a life. Is not the real life of a human that of being able to devote oneself to one's occupation, enjoying it, forgetting the difference between one's private and one's working life. This is indeed the real reward." Not everyone can feel the enthusiasm of a man like Sazo Idemitsu: but nearly everyone can receive some stimulus in being part of a group achieving joint objectives.

33

It must be remembered that human beings existed for hundreds of thousands of years as hunter gatherers, when people worked together in communities comprising the family, the village or the tribe. Humans have thus inherited an instinct to enjoy working in groups in pursuit of common objectives. Consequently it is an error to assume that only the artist or craftsman working on his own can enjoy his work. On the contrary this is actually easier for groups of people, provided they are free to choose their own objectives and their own leaders.

The Difficulty

In conventional industry it is virtually impossible for workers to discover what balance of satisfactions will best fulfil their lives. It is a fallacy to assume that progress in human affairs can be arranged by ordinary people. It is only their leaders who can devise detailed measures of improvement, because it is only they who have all the facts at their disposal and only they who have the power to try out different arrangements. All that the people themselves can do is, firstly to decide what they like and what they don't, and secondly to get rid of leaders who fail to give them what they like. Individuals can of course make suggestions: but they are rarely in possession of enough of the facts to be able to see all the possible results and repercussions of any particular proposal — which (incidentally) is why it is impractical to conduct government by referendum.

Unfortunately trade union leaders lack the business details which would enable them to assess the financial effects of any particular measures designed to give their members more meaningful work. In considering (for example) the question of improving workers' skills — how could a trade union negotiator effectively propose training schemes, which management would probably oppose, the operation of which would depend on management, the effect of which would only be long term, and the (unknown) cost of which would result in reduced wages? This is but one example of the impossibility of workers, or their present leaders, finding out what balance between meaningful achievement and pay will best fulfil their working lives.

Some people will say that ordinary workers would never have the sense to forego cash in order to better their working skills: but, on the contrary, this is precisely what they do (in a big way) in the established worker-ownership organisations. For details see 'Education, Welfare, Social' in Chapter 13. What workers lack in conventional industry is leaders able to propose and implement the necessary arrangements.

It follows that, if people at work are to achieve the real object of work, which is their personal fulfilment, their leaders must be their business managers. There is no other way in which it is possible for them even to discover what they want. It further follows that people are never going to

34

achieve the happiness which is possible for them at work until the capital ownership system is replaced by a system of worker-ownership.

The State

It is necessary to refute ideas that the state has any duty to interfere with worker-owners seeking their own fulfilment in their own enterprises, as follows:

Firstly, appropriate regulations will protect the public from such dangers as noise, pollution, monopoly, misrepresentation, and general financial skulduggery.

Secondly, a market protects consumers because it compels producers to please them. It is sometimes contended that manufacturers induce consumers to buy inferior products by means of advertising. However, if it pleases people to buy something which looks good in a glossy advert, why should they be denied this pleasure? We are all us liable to find pleasure in being (what other people call) 'silly'. The essential point is that, in a free market, producers can only get money out of consumers by giving them pleasure.

Thirdly, in a worker-ownership system the government need no longer be concerned with the efficiency of individual business enterprises, because the GNP (gross national product) becomes of secondary importance. Instead of depending on their government, different collections of people at work decide the amount of their own consumption by means of their own production.*

Summary

People at work seek other important satisfactions, such as meaningful achievement, besides that of earning money. Since the balance they prefer varies with different people in different circumstances, we can only say that the object of work is the fulfilment of the worker. By contrast, people who supply capital to industry simply seek to make money. The more a business succeeds in making money, the more these two objectives diverge.

Given control of their own work, people could make their business enterprises into mutual benefit societies of human beings, in which work would be a fulfilling occupation. However, lacking this control, people have

---

* It is natural for people to wish to better their conditions. Indeed, since this is the mainspring of human progress, it is known as 'divine discontent'. However, if we work for wages, we only have two means of betterment. One is a higher level of wages, and the other is more government hand-outs. These are, therefore, what we demand. Unforunately the government can only comply with our demands if there is an increase in the production of goods and services. Hence the cry that we must all work harder and more efficiently — whether we really all want to do so or not.

no means of even discovering what balance of satisfactions will best fulfil them.

Given a market economy and appropriate regulations, the state has no reason to interfere in the ways in which different collections of worker-owners pursue their own fulfilment.

"Unemployment"

4 — Unemployment

*". . . because he knows a frightful fiend doth close behind him
tread." — S. T. Coleridge*

Synopsis

A Necessary Evil is how we regard unemployment.

Unemployment is unnecessary in developed nations.

Token Money is used in the exchange of goods and services.

The Cause of unemployment is over-pricing.

Recessions result from a decrease in the money supply without a corresponding decrease in the amount of money paid out to producers.

Eastern Europe demonstrates full employment.

The Problem is how to get people at work to accept as their reward the current monetary value of what they produce.

Low Earnings do not result from worker-ownership.

The Poor will be better rather than worse off.

Other Objections are invalid.

A Necessary Evil

We take for granted such 'necessary evils' as unrequited love and the common cold. We may not all suffer them, but we accept their incidence. This was how people in the past looked on the incidence of sabre-toothed tigers. We now wonder how they could have lived with such a danger: but they did so because they had to. We live with the danger of unemployment for the same reason. Of course we try to avoid it, just as our ancestors tried to avoid being eaten by a sabre-toothed tiger: but we, like them, regard its possibility as a necessary evil. In reality however, unemployment in developed countries today is evil without being necessary.

We tolerate unemployment only because we have a misleading picture of industry. In this picture we see industry and trade as operations in which workers produce goods and services for sale to consumers. Employment can thus only be available for workers to the extent that consumers have enough money with which to buy what workers produce: and it is obvious that there must be some limit to the amount of money which consumers will have available in any given period. Indeed there is now discussion of the need for

39

people to learn to enjoy leisure, on the grounds that industry will soon be able to produce more goods and services than consumers can ever buy.

In these circumstances it seems that each nation has to make careful plans to maintain employment, and that international arrangements are needed to coordinate these. There is much disagreement between people on the measures to be adopted: but everyone accepts the fact that to do nothing is to do something definitely wrong. Unemployment is like a tiger lying in wait for societies which do not plan to avoid it.

Since these views are quite widely held, it is important to explain that the whole picture painted above is an illusion. Trade and industry are not really processes of production and sale. Remuneration of productive work is not limited by the availability of money. On the contrary it is production which limits consumption. Gainful employment is potentially available for everyone in developed countries. We suffer unemployment, not because we fail to take measures to avoid it, but because we operate a system which induces it. Unemployment in developed nations is the natural result of a system of capital control of work.

Unemployment

In the past, unemployment resulted from limitations of food and transport. When food is short people will only exchange their goods for food. When transport is limited it is difficult for people, both to get raw materials and to convey their produce to those who want it. In those circumstances the only certain way of having work was to own land capable of growing food. However in developed countries today such conditions no longer apply. So many different materials and processes are now available that people can produce an immense variety of goods and services, all of which are able to be transported to other people who want them. The problem for the citizens of developed countries today is merely that of deciding which forms of production will best provide them with fulfilment at work.

Token Money

Although we appear to buy and sell goods and services, what we really do is to exchange them. Money is only a token which avoids the need for barter. When we give someone our produce he gives us money in exchange, which enables us to get the particular goods or services we want from some other producer. The reality of trade and industry is thus, not production and sale, but production and exchange. If all the money in the world disappeared tomorrow, we could all go on exchanging goods and services — using cowrie shells instead of dollars.

It might be thought, nevertheless, that our ability to exchange our produce would depend on there being enough other producers with whom to make the exchange. Happily there is no such problem. When we offer our goods or services for exchange, what we do (in effect) is to put them into a local or national or international market: and it is the property of a market that the more goods and services which are put into it, the more there are to take out. It follows that, if we put our production into an appropriate market, we can always be sure of getting out of the market an equivalent amount of other people's production. This applies irrespective of the size of the market — the only advantage of a large market being a bigger variety of produce from which to choose.*

Of course we must produce something which is wanted by other people. A market will not dispose of white elephants. Also of course we must choose a product which is easily transportable to the appropriate market. It is no good producing concrete blocks in the middle of the Sahara. And of course we must keep an eye on the market so as to avoid producing something already over-supplied. Even so that leaves literally thousands of different goods and services available for production, which can be transported to people who want them and which, therefore, have an exchange value.

Some people may object that, as production increases, so will prices fall and workers get less money for what they produce: but of course it is goods and services, not money, which matters. The more goods and services which are produced the more there are available for everyone. There is only one proviso, which is that each lot of producers can only get out of the market the current exchange value of what they put in.

The Cause

Unemployment, of a long term nature, thus arises only because people are unwilling to exchange their produce for its market value. Nothing wanted by other people is unsaleable. It is just a question of the price of what is offered.* When a business manager says that he cannot find a 'market' for his produce, what he really means is that he cannot find anyone willing to agree his valuation of his produce. In the end practically all non-perishable goods get sold off at some price or other, even if at a much lower figure than originally intended. The difficulty is that, if the production of such goods is to

---

*This is a provable theorem, which can be tested algebraically. However, if the reader has forgotten his algebra, he can satisfy himself by considering a very small market of (say) 3 people. Calculations will be easier if the reader starts by assuming that these people all produce the same quantity of goods with the same value (i.e. which they all equally want). The reader can then try increasing and decreasing both the number of producers and the amounts and the values of the goods which they put into the market: but, whatever he does, he will find that each producer always gets out of the market the precise value of what he puts in. The only variation is that the exchange value of each product rises and falls according to the amount of it put into the market.

*"What is offered" is here taken to include the advertising, the packaging, the 'mark-up' to wholesalers and retailers, the extent of distribution, the way the goods are displayed and the general degree of effort made to please the customer.

41

continue, it may be necessary to lower the wages (and the profits) concerned. If that is not acceptable, then the workers concerned become unemployed.

It follows that workers could always find a business able to employ them if they would accept as their reward their portion of the market value of what that business produces.* Unfortunately this is not a practical possibility in a democratic state with the conventional system of industrial ownership. When work is controlled by capital, in an otherwise free society, there will always be a demand for minimum wages. However it is inevitable that different businesses, with different managers and different collections of workers, will operate with differing degrees of efficiency. Consequently, if minimum wages are fixed high enough to give workers a 'fair' share of the earnings of most businesses, those wages will be too high for atleast some (actual or potential) businesses to pay. The workers concerned will then be unemployed.

Recessions

The problem is aggravated by variations in the amount of money. Since money is a token for goods and services, it provides a convenient means of saving these up. Normally the saving and spending of money by people engaged in exchanging goods and services balances out: but it is obvious that there are liable to be periods when all concerned save or spend rather more or rather less money. A 'business recession' is a period in which spending is reduced. Cause and effect then operate in the following manner:

- The amount of money in circulation becomes less, but the amount of goods and services being produced and exchanged remains remains the same. The monetary value of goods and services is thus reduced.
- This has no practical effect on the rewards available for work because, although people are payed less money for what they produce, they pay out less money for what they get in exchange, i.e. although wages and profits fall, so do prices.
- However the wage earners fail to see this — so they refuse to accept less money for their work — so they become unemployed.
- This reduces the amount of goods and services being produced, which results in a real (as opposed to an imaginary) reduction in wealth.
- With luck, the reduction in goods and services then matches the reduction in money, so that prices rise again. People then go back to work, and real wealth starts to increase again.
- Until it happens all over again!

*Of course this assumes that workers with redundant skills are retrained, which is not guaranteed to happen at present: but, it will be seen in Chapter 13 (under 'Education, Welfare, Social') that training for workers is accorded enormously increased importance in conditions of worker-ownership.

Governments can halt this sequence of events, by adopting the Keynesian technique of deliberate inflationary borrowing: but there are difficulties explained in Appendix F.

Eastern Europe

The evidence that unemployment is unnecessary is provided by Eastern Europe. A member of the Hungarian workers co-operative organisation remarked to the author that "of course a man would never remain unemployed here, as he might do in your country". When the new communist regimes were set up in Eastern Europe after the war, one of their first objectives was to provide employment for everyone: and, by the 1970s, they had all succeeded in doing this. Consequently, when unemployment (and inflation) hit the Western nations, those in Eastern Europe suffered from neither.

The dictatorships in Eastern Europe maintain full employment by the simple process of limiting wages. The amounts of money paid out in wages are made to match the amounts of money achieved by sales, even where the need for exports requires sales to be made at free market prices. Unfortunately this cure for unemployment requires a degree of state control of industry which results in inefficient production. Most people in the West thus find the cure worse than the disease.

The Problem

The problem of maintaining full employment is that of persuading people at work in different businesses to accept as their reward the market value of the goods or services produced by their business. A 'wages policy' cannot achieve this, because of the point (explained above) that there are sure to be some enterprises unable to pay a wage level considered 'fair' for most. This problem is resolved in Eastern Europe by dictatorial limitation of wages to the same level for all, with the result that the more efficient enterprises effectively subsidise the wages paid in the less efficient ones. Since this would not be acceptable in the democracies, it is difficult to see how any 'wages policy' could be designed which would produce full employment.

The solution is obvious. Let people at work have control of their own work in their own businesses. When workers are thus assured, firstly that they control the policies of their business, and secondly that they get all its net earnings, it will seem obvious and just that their reward should be the exchange value of what they produce.

Although of secondary importance, a system of worker-ownership will also put an end to certain bad practices which arise in the system of capital ownership.

43

- It is a principle of conventional economics that, when a business cannot pay 'minimum' wages, it closes down and its workers are left to move to more successful enterprises. This involves mobility of labour, which is nice for economists but not always so nice for the workers concerned. In a worker-ownership system people will be able to avoid being made redundant and having to move, by accepting lower rewards for a period whilst they take steps to increase the earning capacity of their existing business.
- It is also a principle of conventional economics that a business which can only sell part of its production (at the required price) shall dismiss part of its work force: so that those workers who remain may continue to draw minimum wages. However most workers would prefer an arrangement in which all accepted lower earnings for a period, in order that all might remain at work. This is made possible by worker-ownership.
- Employers often now pay overtime, as a means of giving workers more money without any permanent commitment to higher wages. However overtime as a regular practice is bad for people at work. In worker-ownership conditions the device is unnecessary.

Low Earnings

Trade union officials often fear that a system of worker-ownership will enable people to work for low remuneration. It does indeed do so. However minimum wage rates are only required to prevent employers from paying workers less than is in fact available. That danger no longer arises when workers become the owners of all their business assets. If they elect to draw out less of their own money than corresponds to minimum wage rates, they will only do so if (in their judgement) this will benefit them in the long run.

It is also feared that low rewards accepted by worker-owners will tend to lower the rewards (wages) of all workers, because worker-owners will be able to undercut prices. However this overlooks the point that workers are also consumers: so that reductions in wages which also have the effect of reducing prices do them no harm. Their wages will still buy them the same amount of goods and sevices as before.

Even so, it is feared that low wages and low prices benefit the rich (who do no work) disproportionately. This may be true of our present system: but, in worker-ownership conditions, whatever riches industry may produce accrue to those who produce them. Any rich people will thus be either workers or ex-workers. (The point is further considered under 'Capital Creation' in Chapter 6.)

The Poor

It is also feared that, when people only get the value of what they produce, less able people will be worse off than under a capital-ownership system coupled with minimum wages. This tends to overlook the point (made above) that people in a business can never be rewarded with more goods and services than they produce. There are thus only two ways in which an individual can be paid more money than he earns. One is for the 'differentials' in a business to be limited, so that the less able workers are (in effect) subsidised by the abler ones. The other is for the owners of a business to allocate more of its earnings to the less able workers than their work contribution is worth — which is much the same thing.

It cannot be doubted that, whatever is done under the above heads now, will be better done in worker-ownership conditions. One of the first things new worker-owners tend to consider is a limit on differentials. Consequently the less able members of society will be better (rather than worse) treated in worker-ownership conditions.

Other Objections

It may be thought that circumstances are bound to arise in which a worker-owned business is caught by a major reduction in demand for its products, with the result that its members become unemployed just like those of a comparable capitalist business. The fact that this is not so is explained under 'Job Security' in Chapter 13 and in Appx M "Full Employment".

It may be contended that minimum wages are not the only cause of unemployment and that is this just as likely to arise from job changing, from changes in the pattern of trade and from cyclical and volatile demand. However none of these need seriously contribute to unemployment.

- In the 1960s there was a period in the South of England when unemployment fell below 2%. As this figure included everyone changing jobs, that factor cannot be a serious contribution to unemployment. Further (as explained in Chapter 13) job changing is much reduced in worker-ownership conditions.
- Dislocation of trade does cause unemployment: but the example of Germany after the last war shows how quickly this can be overcome when the will exists. In Germany, the factories had been destroyed, the economy was in chaos and there was a flood of refugees from the East: and yet work was rapidly found by everyone.
- The building trade exemplifies cyclical demand, which conventional building trade employers like to meet by taking on and laying off workers. However it is quite common for manufacturers to run several lines of production, so that they can switch from one to another as demand varies. Worker-owners apply this practice to both cyclical and volatile demand. In addition they are able (if it suits them) to accept low earnings in times of low demand for their product in order to get the advantage of high earnings in times of high demand.

The matter is further considered under 'Job Security' in Chapter 13 and in Appendix M — Full Employment.

Summary

We look on (some degree of) unemployment as a necessary evil. This is because we picture trade and industry as processes of production and sale, with production dependent on the availability of buyers. In reality trade is a process of exchange, and a market will always exchange goods which anyone wants.

Production, and hence employment, is thus only limited by the willingness of workers to accept as their reward the market value of what they produce. They are deterred from doing this by minimum wages, particularly during a 'recession'. We see in Eastern Europe how control of wages can produce full employment.

In a democracy, no wages policy can provide full employment because of the different earning capacity of different enterprises. However people in worker-owned businesses will readily accept the value of what they produce as a fair reward for their work. Such a system (besides resulting in full employment) will provide workers with more, rather than less, rewards than they get now. Similarly the less able members of society will be better, rather than worse, off.

The matter is further considered under 'Job Security' in Chapter 13 and in Appendix M — Full Employment.

"The Market"

48

5 — The Market

"Vae victis" — Livy*

Synopsis

The Problem of a market is that, whilst it is good for consumers, it damages workers.

Market Advantages are twofold.

Business Growth naturally advantages capitalist owners.

Market Competition is thus distorted in a capital-ownership system.

The Remedy is to restore the natural operation of a market by means of worker-ownership.

The Problem

In the past, it was accepted that a market was the natural way of exchanging goods and services. Since the industrial revolution, however, a view has arisen which condemns the market. There are now two opinions. One condemns the market as damaging workers, whilst the other condemns lack of a market as damaging consumers. As often happens when views are strongly held, each side tends to exaggerate its case. Anti-marketeers thus contend that a market does not really benefit consumers, whilst pro-marketeers discount the damage it does to workers. In fact a market does damage workers and lack of it does damage consumers.

Let us first consider damage to workers. This takes the form of redundancy resulting from a business being unable to market its goods. Thus (for example) a man may have given many years of faithful service to a business. Suddenly he is told he is to be made redundant, not for any personal reason, but because market demand has changed. The unfortunate man suddenly finds himself deprived of a livelihood through no fault of his own.

Of course most societies now take action to soften the blow. In Britain, the man will get a capital payment plus 'unemployment benefit' until he can find another job.† However, even if he gets another job immediately, he will have to leave companions with whom he has built up a mutual relationship: whilst in most cases he will face an unknown period of unemployment with all the worry and uncertainty which that involves, possibly only ending (if it ends at all) with the necessity of moving house and family.*

*Which may be freely translated as "devil take the hindmost".
†However these measures are necessarily a compromise. In justice, what the redundant worker ought to get is full pay whilst unemployed, plus a capital sum for disturbance. Unfortunately any reasonable level of unemployment benefit is bound to discourage some people from working, and any capital payments can discourage workers from trying to save a business in difficulty.

In these circumstances, is it surprising that people have sought the (illusory) safety of state ownership? Is it surprising that they demand ever bigger compensation for job loss and ever bigger 'doles' for those out of work. Is it surprising that they condemn a market economy?

Market Advantages

We make the best use of our work capacity if we integrate it with that of others: and the point has been made in Chapter 2 that men working together cab literally 'move mountains'. However, in a free society in a free society we hold that the individual need only work in the ways and to the extent that he chooses. How then do we get people to integrate their work in the most effective manner, without appling compulsion to them?

This is what the market does. In effect the market says to people in their capacity as producers — "Do what you like. Stay in bed all day if you prefer. However, in so far as you want any goods or services from your neighbours, you must produce goods or services for them." At the same time it it says to people in their capacity as consumers — "Buy what you like or buy nothing at all: but, whatever you do choose to buy, you must pay for." In this way the market, without applying compulsion to anyone, arranges for the work done by producers to be precisely what most pleases consumers. The market even arranges 'service with a smile'.

The market also does something which can be done effectively by no other means. This is to value goods and services. It must be borne in mind that there is no such thing as 'intrinsic value'. Values are a matter of supply and demand, and therefore constantly changing. How then do we determine the comparative values of all the goods and services currently available? Let us take (for example) — on the one hand a man's shirt of a given size, colour and quality, available in a shop in a particular locality, where the assistants serve customers with a given degree of speed and help — and on the other hand a ticket for a theatre in another locality, in a particular seat, of a given degree of comfort, for the performance of a particular play, with certain actors, at a given time. How do we compare the value of these two items?

The market does this without requiring us to do any more than spend our money as we choose. No forms need be filled in. No army of civil servants is required to collate the information. Indeed no civil service could ever produce the information in time for it to be of any use. The shortages and queues we see behind the Iron Curtain mostly arise, not because the planners give precedence to guns over butter, but because they constantly get the prices wrong. Indeed they would hardly know where to begin if they could not look out at the markets of the free world.

Anti-marketeers claim that the complexities of modern industry prevent the market from serving consumers effectively. However anyone who travels about the world soon sees how much better consumers are served in market economies. The only people who doubt this are those who have never experienced 'planned economies'.

Business Growth

Since theory predicates that a market benefits both producers and consumers, and since this was always so in the past, we need to know what has gone wrong now. The damage which a market does stems from the collection of workers into competing enterprises in the factory age. In these conditions, business growth almost always benefits capitalist business owners. Such owners depend for their reward on a margin of profit remaining over after their business has met all its liabilities, including that of wage payments. They naturally hope to get the best profit possible per worker employed.* However it was soon discovered that capitalist owners get much more money by taking a small margin of profit off a lot of workers in a large business, than by trying to get a large margin per worker in a small business. This is why business growth is automatically equated with business success. The classic success story is one in which an entrepreneur starts with two men and a boy in a shed and ends up with a vast factory employing hundreds of people.

Growth is thus the normal objective of a business: and this naturally results in a fierce struggle for sales. If the average capitalist business is not actually planning to expand its market, it will at least be trying to avoid losing it. In this constant battle for sales, the weakest naturally go to the wall. That is unfortunate: but it is a situation freely accepted by the kind of people who choose to become business operators. However it is not a situation which ordinary workers enjoy at all. They cannot make their fortunes in a successful business, but they can be mde redundantin an unsuccessful one. They thus have a lot to lose and not much to gain.

Market Competition

In the days of village industry, those workers who served customers best got the most money. People paid more for the shoes made by the better cobblers. However that did not stop the other cobblers from working. They just got less for their shoes. The first difference nowadays is that a cobbler is no longer (in effect) a business partner, getting paid according to the customer's valuation of the shoes produced, but a factory worker getting a trade union wage. The second difference is that the more cobblers a factory owner can employ the more profits he is likely to make.

Let us take an imaginary example of two boot and shoe making businesses, Firm A and Firm B, which divide the market for footwear between them: and

*To be precise, capitalists want the best possible profit per unit of equity capital employed: and, of course, they seek business expansion without the introduction of additional equity capital. Managers also normally seek growth, as a means of extending their 'empires'. However they are only allowed to pursue this aim because the result is to benefit their capitalist masters.

let us suppose that Firm A discovers how to produce footwear slightly better or cheaper than Firm B. In such circumstances it would be reasonable if the owners of Firm A made slightly more profit than those of Firm B. However that is not what happens in our present economy. What Firm A does is to market either better shoes at the same price or the same shoes at a lower price. The result, if this continues, is to put Firm B out of business whilst Firm A doubles in size — probably taking on many of Firm B's workers.

What is wrong with this situation is that the rewards of success and the penalties of failure are out of all proportion to the variations in efficiency of production. "So much the better for consumers", it may be said: but even that is not necessarily true, because the damage done to the workers (through their being made redundant) repercusses in ways which eventually damage consumers too. One way, for example, is when the workers demand an end to the market.

The Remedy

What the workers fail to see is that they are damaged, not because they take part in a market system, but because they are excluded from it. In a capital ownership system a market functions, not between consumers and producers, but between consumers and capitalist business owners. As we see, this distorts the natural functioning of a market. The remedy is to make workers into business owners, when the market will function normally again.

Worker-owners obtain no automatic advantage from enlargement of a business because, although more workers produce more earnings, they also produce more owners to share those earnings. What worker-owners want therefore is, not increased sales, but the same sales at a higher price (or a lower cost). It is true that even a worker-owned business may seek expansion in order to reach its optimum operating size: but it is explained in Chapter 13 how this is more likely to be done by close cooperation between existing enterprises, than by their individual expansion.

Even so, it may be feared that worker-ownership will be less effective in serving consumers. In fact the reverse is more likely. At present the owners (and hence the managers) of a business are very strongly motivated to please consumers, because the rewards of success are large and the penalties of failure severe. However the people who actually do the work are hardly motivated at all. In worker-ownership conditions the motivation to provide consumers with what they want may be less, but it is applied to everyone in the business. The capital-ownership system may have worked well in the past, when workers were expected to do as they were told: but systems dependent on compulsion are no longer as effective as they were. It is really a matter of dictatorship versus democracy. For the people of 'advanced' nations, democracy (although it may sometimes creak a bit) is the more effective system of the two.

52

The way in which competition operates in the changed circumstances of worker-ownership is explained, in relation to Firms A and B above, in Appendix G — The Uncompetitive Market.

Summary

Current disagreement about the market is due to the fact that, whilst market operations benefit consumers, they damage workers. This is caused by the distortion of normal market functioning in a capital ownership system.

Damage to workers arises from the fact that capitalist business owners have found, since the industrial revolution, that they almost always benefit from business expansion. Hence the demand for growth, which results in fierce competition for sales. In this sales battle, workers on fixed wages gain little if their enterprises win but face redundancy if they lose.

Worker-owners by contrast, since they get no automatic advantage from expansion of their business, do not compete for sales and thus have no incentive to damage each other. The remedy therefore is to restore the market to normal operation by means of a system of worker-ownership. On balance this will not result in consumers being any less well served.

A further explanation appears as 'Three Fairy Tales' in Appendix H.

"Capital & Labour"

6 — Capital & Labour

"How happy is he born and taught that serveth not another's will" — Sir Henry Wotton

Synopsis

Stored Labour is how we can describe capital.

Social Damage arises when an individual foregoes the right to create his own.

Capital Creation by people at work should accrue to themselves.

Capital Reward is necessary for those who make it available to others.

Source of Capital is the saving of business earnings.

Stored Labour

We think of capital as money: but capital is really the goods and services which money represents. Since goods and services are produced by labour, capital comprises the results of labour which have been stored up instead of being expended. Men's ability to store up the fruits of their labour is the main cause of their pre-eminence amongst the animals. When men were hunters and gatherers, they had to work nearly every day simply to get food. Agriculture was a great advance because it enabled men to grow food during one period and eat it in the next. Nowadays we can not only grow crops and keep animals, but we can store up foodstuffs in cans and packets and frozen foods. However the really important use of capital began when a man learned how to make a spear one week and use it in the next week's hunting. By this means puny man was able to match the teeth and claws of otherwise more powerful predators. As a result the main use of capital is in combination with work. We now make complex machines in one period which we combine with work in the next period, so that the work may then involve no more than pressing a button.

When capital and labour are viewed in this light we see how odd it is that we should talk of a partnership between them. Labour is people currently at work; whereas capital is the result of past work, by people who may well be dead. Capital must obviously be bought or hired from those who have created or acquired it: but that is no reason for their being given control of the work which makes use of the capital. The picture may be clearer if we 'go back to the land'.

Not so long ago a young farmer, after cultivating his fields, might use up his surplus energy in breaking up an adjacent piece of moorland. After a time he would have produced an entirely new arable field, where nothing but

55

heather had existed before. He would thus have created for himself a new capital asset. However, as the years went by, he would have grown old and found his farm too big for him. If he had no sons of the right age, he might have said to a young man nearby "how about you cultivating this extra field of mine, which is becoming too much for me?" Naturally the young man would expect to make some payment for the use of an extra field: so he would have either bought or rented it from the older man. Either way, the young man would still have been free to create new arable land for himself.

Social Damage

The above was obviously satisfactory: but there was an alternative arrangement available to the old man. He could have offered to employ the younger man to work for him for a fixed fee — a wage. That arrangement might be thought equally satisfactory: but, if the young man thus gave up control of his own labour, he lost any opportunity of creating capital for himself in his turn. He thus, to a degree, enslaved himself. "Well", it may be asked, "if the young man agreed, why should we question his choice? It was his affair." However the problem is that any form of enslavement is judged bad for society, whether it is freely entered into or not.

Not so long ago a man might have been defeated in battle and, as a result, offered the choice of slavery or death. If he chose slavery, he could not complain at his lot thereafter. We forego this practice nowadays, not because we never fight and take prisoners, but because we regard the presence of slaves in society as undesirable. This applies to any degree of slavery. In India, in the past, there existed whole villages controlled by the local money-lender, because the villagers owed him so much that they could never repay him. A villager often lacked the money for the marriage feast of a daughter: so he borrowed on terms which made repayment virtually impossible. The arrangements were freely agreed: but, since the result was judged bad for society, laws were made to restrict them. We apply the same principle in bankruptcy laws today. After a period of time, the bankrupt is allowed to escape from his creditors, not because this is equitable, but in order to avoid his enslavement.

Our arrangements about inventions have the same basis. We encourage the activities of inventors because they benefit us all. For this purpose we have patent laws: but a patent for an invention is granted only for a limited number of years. Otherwise we might still be paying royalties to the descendants of that clever Chinese who first invented the wheel. The idea is that a patent right should last long enough to provide an inventor with substantial benefit, but not so long that the the rest of society begins to be enslaved by the need to pay royalties to him.

Capital Creation

Many ordinary workers look on successful industrialists as people who live on the backs of the workers. This is largely a myth. The successful business man is usually the inventor of some plan or process which makes two blades of grass grow where one grew before. He has found some way of producing more or better or cheaper goods or services. If he benefits from so doing, his benefit comes from new wealth created by himself. Such people should be encouraged by society because, however much they may grow rich they benefit us all in the process. We are unwise, as well as unjust, if we penalise them in any way.

Unfortunately the capital ownership system positively encourages those who thus create capital to use it thereafter to enslave their fellow workers. Thus (for example) a gentleman called Herr Zeiss benefited us all by inventing the prismatic binocular, for which he was very properly granted patent rights. In due course those rights expired: but, by that time, the people whom Herr Zeiss had been able to employ had evolved new techniques which enabled the Zeiss business to go on making money. However this additional money went — and still goes — not to the discoverers of the further new processes, but to the heirs and assigns of Herr Zeiss.

Another instance is that of the old time prospector who struck oil. No one begrudged him his new found riches, because these comprised wealth which had not previously been available to anyone. However it soon became necessary to employ people to operate the more complicated processes of oil extraction: so that, today, the successors of the old time prospectors are the great oil companies. As a result, although people still strike oil, those who do so are seldom enriched in the process. They just draw wages and salaries, whilst the increased riches go to the stockholders of the oil companies.

In the capital-ownership system, as it has been evolved, a young man who inherits wealth can continue to increase that wealth without himself contributing anything to society. He need not even be clever to do this. All he requires is a modicum of common sense in paying for skilled advice. In other words the old adage that money begets money is perfectly correct. It is this aspect of the system which divides society into the haves and the have-nots, the rich and the poor, the capitalists and the workers.

This is of course why most democratic societies enact taxation which discriminates against the rich. People have a feeling — which we see to be often correct — that the rich somehow get their money unfairly. However extra taxation of the rich is a very blunt weapon, because it hits genuine inventors and innovators equally with those who have done nothing useful for their increased capital. A system of worker-ownership would, by contrast, correct the matter at source.

Capital Reward

It might appear from the above that worker-ownership is planned as an anti-capitalist reform. This is not so because, in denying them the means of risk-taking investment, worker-ownership will deprive ordinary capitalists of nothing which they need. We tend to muddle up capitalists and industrialists. People with spare money and people with managerial ability are two quite different sets of persons.

Business directors and managers (industrialists) comprise a small minority of citizens, who have both the desire and the ability to run things. If they also like innovation and risk, they may become risk taking entrepreneurs. Like very brave men in battle, we admire such people without necessarily wishing to emulate them. Capitalists on the other hand (as has been explained in Chapter 1) comprise nearly all of us: and very few of us find it important to be able to invest our money at risk in order to make capital gains. What ordinary people want is to get some return on any spare money (capital) they happen to possess. Most people will thus be perfectly happy with a system in which industry is financed only by loan capital. A minority of people are now used to buying equity shares for capital appreciation, and they would feel deprived if this possibility was suddenly removed. However, if the future possessors of spare cash find themselves in a society in which capital is only rewarded with rates of fixed interest, they will suffer no ill. Similarly, the notion of a stock exchange dealing only in fixed interest securities may seem horrifying to existing 'city men': but it will not worry their descendants.

Source of Capital

Many people imagine capital as a commodity held by banks, from whom it has to be acquired by the operators of industry. Such people are inclined to think that it would be better if the government held the capital and distributed it according to need. In reality capital is created by industry, and most of the capital used by business enterprises is that which has been created by themselves through reinvestment of their business earnings. Some capital is also created by individuals who save their earnings, and these are made available to industry by institutions like banks. Market processes thus provide the owners of capital with a return on their money, and industry with a source of borrowing. Nevertheless some people object to capital in private hands and dislike its allocation to industry by market processes.

Objections to market processes are misguided. As with the economy in general, the market operates far better than could any government agency. Firstly, the market discovers the current general need for capital and encourages or discourages its creation accordingly by setting general interest rates.* Secondly, the market determines the appropriate rates to be paid for

*Although these can be varied by the particular policies of different nations.

borrowing capital in varying circumstances, i.e. large or small amounts, long or short term, possible degree of risk and so forth. Thirdly, the market channels capital to those who can make best of use of it, by giving it to those who will pay most for it. It is only government departments who give capital to people who are likely to lose it.

Objections to private capital will be equally misguided, once we cease to operate a system which enables (indeed encourages) the owners of capital to enslave their fellow citizens. When capital accrues only to those who create it by their work, and when it no longer gives them power to employ others, there will be no harm in its ownership by individuals. Further, the acquirement of capital will be partly a matter of choice: and people who choose to forego other satisfactions in order to make more money should be free to enjoy the fruits of their choice.

Summary

Capital is stored labour. A man who uses his labour to create capital, and then makes that capital available to others, is entitled to be paid for it. However the capital ownership system provides the owners of capital with the means of employing others for wages. The wage earners then create capital, not for themselves, but for their employers. This is bad for society because it is, even when freely agreed, a form of enslavement.

One of its effects is to enable the owners of capital to increase their capital without themselves working. This is the reason for differential taxation of the rich. However that taxation discourages initiative because it falls as much on those who create capital with their own labour, as on those who acquire it by means of other people's labour. The answer is to change from capital ownership, in which system people are mostly compelled to work for wages, to worker-ownership, in which system the owners of capital cannot 'employ' people. In these circumstances private ownership of capital will be harmless.

"The Two Doctors"

7 — Politics

"The important thing for government is, not to do things which individuals are doing already, and to do them a little better or a little worse, but to do those things which at present are not being done at all" — J.M. Keynes

Synopsis

The Two Doctors are the politicians of Left and Right.

Left and Right need to reconsider their opinions.

Taxation for the redistribution of wealth is bad.

Democracy is best on a hierarchical basis.

The Two Doctors

Political views tend to be polarised between Left and Right. People with Left wing views see that things are wrong with society: but they fail to see the cause and consequently propose the wrong remedies. People with Right wing views fail to see anything so particularly wrong: and they thus concentrate on opposing the mistaken policies of the Left. The politicians are like two doctors treating a patient with pain in his lower limbs. This pain makes walking difficult for the patient. However he has an excellent pair of trade union crutches which enable him to carry on with his work, although they do nothing to cure whatever is wrong with him. The picture then is as follows —

- The Left wing doctor, seeing the patient suffering, prescribes various 'welfare' drugs to relieve the pains.
- The Right wing doctor acquiesces: but he is worried that these drugs are bad for the patient's general health.
- Both doctors agree on the patient's use of his trade union crutches: but, whereas the Left wing doctor wants these made as strong as possible, the Right wing doctor wants them to be kept light enough not to impede the patient's work. Given strong enough crutches, the patient is liable to use them to hit his doctors over the head if they fail to give him enough of the welfare drugs.
- The two doctors tend to dispute about the amount of welfare drugs to be given to the patient. The Left wing doctor wants to give more and the Right wing doctor less. The Left wing doctor regards his colleague as a callous brute who does not really mind the patient suffering, whilst the Right wing doctor thinks the other a fool who will end by killing the patient. If there happens to be a third doctor available, his views are predictably half way between the other two.

- The patient tends to consult his doctors alternately, without giving them time either to kill or cure him.
- What neither of the doctors has discovered is that the patient's pains arise from his having adopted a wrong position at work, as a result of which he has a slipped disc in his spine. If the patient will change his position at work, his disc will gradually return to normal, the pains in his lower limbs will cease and he can throw away his trade union crutches.

Left and Right

Those readers with Left wing views are urged to consider the following views of a Yugoslav writer:

"One important reason (for advocating state control) is the intellectual's illusion that he can make society operate more rationally and justly if he has all the power centralised in his hands. He lets himself believe that society is like a laboratory and he is the benevolent scientist, who will set everything right and will solve problems scientifically. We have learned, however, that the individual never knows enough to run society humanely and rationally from the centre, no matter how great his power. For he attempts to explain each of his failures by the liberties someone else has taken, spoiling his plan. People do not act or react in the way the authoritarian expects them to do: but, because he lays the fault to them instead of to himself, his idea of a remedy is to gain even greater control over them."

"In our view Socialism cannot be created by merely assuming power, nationalising property, and managing the economy in the name of the working people. True Socialism must be democratic, and it cannot be so until Socialist governments solve the problem of putting power into the hands of the ordinary citizen and worker. In attempting to solve this problem the revolutionary government must help him to become a free, competent and responsible agent in social life. Forms must be set up so that he can act on his own to change his living conditions and his economic situation. This cannot be done if we tolerate a bureaucracy with all the power concentrated at the top. Power must be decentralised and decision making brought down to the level of the ordinary citizen and worker. The key then to our thinking is decentralisation, for we believe that rationality and humanism, energetic economic activity and democratic freedom all lie in that direction."

People with Right wing opinions are urged to consider the following statement:

"Conservatives want people to be free and responsible within a market economy. To this end they wish governments to exercise as little control as possible. However people seldom value freedom until they experience it, and they only start to behave responsibly when they are given responsibility. The slave's vision is limited to the idea of a better master who will give him more food and demand less work."

"Conservative ideas can never appeal to people who, in their capacity as producers, are excluded from the market and denied responsibility for their own work. Such people see government power, not as an encroachment on their liberty, but as a curb on that of their masters. Is it any wonder, when people neither control their own work nor obtain any direct benefit from its results, that they seek a 'welfare' society which will look after them from the cradle to the grave? Is it surprising that, instead of demanding freedom to help themselves, their parrot cry is "why doesn't the government do something about it?""

Taxation

As has been explained, the conventional capital ownership system enables 'money to beget money'. Hence high levels of taxation to redistribute wealth. We may think this necessary: but it has many disadvantages

- We encourage capitalists to make money (because this activity provides employment) which we then try and take away from them again by taxation.
- These taxes "fall equally on the just and unjust man".
- The money re-distributed by the government often gives some people too little and others too much. For example, a worker who loses his job through no fault of his own ought to receive full pay, whilst one who fails to look for another job ought to receive nothing!
- Initiative is discouraged. The creators of wealth are discouraged by high taxation and the poor by free hand-outs.
- People are deprived of choice. The rich cannot spend their own money because it goes to provide welfare for the poor, whilst the poor get only those forms of welfare which are chosen by the state.

Finally, the whole process is enormously expensive. It would not be so if taxation was seen by the citizens, firstly as a fair contribution from each in order to pay for common services, and secondly as a small item in their personal budgets. However, when taxation is very high and when people know that much of what they pay will be given away to others, taxpayers are willing to spend time and money in evading taxes. Also the need to raise very large sums of money leads to many different forms of taxation, which involve time spent merely in paying taxes. As a result a whole army of civil servants is required, both to collect the taxes, and to ensure (as far as possible) that they are paid. Indeed, the point is sometimes reached when the cost of collecting a tax exceeds its yield. Then another army of civil servants is required to distribute the welfare and (as far as possible) to ensure that it is not handed out improperly.

It might be thought that the citizens would rebel against this waste of money: but few people class themselves as rich, and people assume that taxes are paid mainly by the rich. They thus vote for higher taxation on the grounds that it is not they who will pay for the 'bread and circuses' it provides. They fail to realise the extent to which high levels of taxation fall indirectly on themselves. They thus enslave themselves to their government by means of their own votes.

The remedy for this evil of high taxation is to distribute business earnings correctly at source. In a system of worker-ownership, firstly all the earnings of a business accrue to its workers, and secondly the distribution of those earnings is democratically decided. Then, anyone who becomes 'rich' will have done so only by the agreement of his fellows and as a result of their joint work. Then also people at work, when they see themselves as the creators of wealth, will realise that nearly all taxation falls ultimately on themselves.* When people as worker-owners see how much they lose by high taxation, they will decide to retain a lot more of their own earnings.

Democracy

At present the operation of political democracy in the Western world suffers from two defects, which worker-ownership will remedy. One defect is lack of a general measure of agreement within national societies: and the other is lack of small enough electoral divisions.

In regard to the first defect, the point has already been made that Western societies are becoming increasingly polarised between the Left and the Right, following the lines of division in industry. Democracy fails to work satisfactorily when people feel themselves divided into two sides. National issues tend to be judged, not on their merits, but on which 'side' benefits most from any particular solution. Thus, after the American civil war, the 'solid South' felt so embittered against the Republicans that it voted Democratic on all occasions, irrespective of the policies involved. An even more extreme case is that of Northern Ireland, in which democracy cannot work at all. It follows that the operation of political democracy will be much improved when there are no longer two sides in industry.

In regard to the second defect, Aldous Huxley wrote — "In a very large and complex society, democracy is almost meaningless except in relation to autonomous groups of manageable size. Small self governing groups are the first condition of responsible democracy." He added that "we are far from Jefferson's ideal of a genuinely free society composed of a hierarchy of self governing groups."

In the past, when people lived in villages or small towns, local problems could be settled locally. Now however thousands of citizens have to vote together for a single member of the legislature. They do not know what he is like before they elect him and, what is worse, they do not know what he has

*For example consumer taxes, which might not appear to affect people as producers, in fact take away money which consumers could otherwise have paid to producers.

done at the end of three or five years as their representative. Nor can the electors at all easily get together to discuss their views.

By contrast, the persons elected to leadership in a worker-owned business are known to all, and their success or failure in directing the business soon becomes apparent to all. Hierarchical democracy thus rises from a secure base.

The members of an enterprise select one of their (tested and proven) leaders to be their representative at the next stage up — the group level. He then joins with the representatives of the other enterprises in the group in electing the directors at that level. Those directors in turn elect the directors at the next level up — probably the national level. At each stage the candidates are known personally to the voters, who are few enough to question them in person and knowledgeable enough of affairs at that level to know what questions to ask.

This system of hierarchical democracy has two important merits. Firstly it gives ordinary people direct control of the daily detail of their lives, which is what most concerns most people. Secondly it enables them to elect representatives in whom they have confidence, to deal with all the wider issues which they themselves have no time to study in detail.

The essential ingredient is trust. In political democracy, people demand systems of direct election for fear that otherwise they will be cheated by those in power: but the practical result is to deprive themselves of all detailed electoral control. Worker-ownership makes available a convenient chain of hierarchical democracy. This could not replace existing political systems, because not everyone works in business enterprises: but it could be made use of.

Summary

The politicians of Left and Right are like two doctors treating a patient for pain in his legs, who do not realise that his pain is caused by a slipped disc, resulting from his working in the wrong position. He can be cured simply by changing his position at work.

The Left should consider the enslaving effect of state control and the Right should consider the enslaving effect of capital ownership.

Re-distribution of wealth by means of taxation is inefficient, often unfair and always very costly. It would be much better for incomes to be democratically decided at source by means of worker-ownership.

Democracy is unsatisfactory when people are divided into capitalists and workers, and when they can only express their will in very large electoral units. Worker-ownership makes industry democratic, provides it with ideal electoral units and removes the capitalists.

"Board of Directors"

8 — Managerial Oligarchy

". . . for it is part of the irony of things that in putting profits above humanity, the employer is in danger of destroying, not only humanity, but the profits themselves" — Appendix C

Synopsis

Managerial Oligarchies may be the way to provide what we want.

State Services can provide people with fulfilment, but only in special circumstances.

Large Businesses can provide people with fulfilment, but —

Business Managers can only do so when their enterprise is prosperous.

General

Notwithstanding what has been written in previous chapters, there do exist organisations in which capital control is so attenuated that policy objectives are decided by management. There are both state services and large business organisations which are so remotely controlled by their capitalist owners that they operate as managerial oligarchies. The objectives of these organisations are largely decided by the management team, the members of which replace themselves only with like-minded persons. A case can be made out to suggest that this method of controlling work will effectively provide workers with fulfilment.

State Services

As explained in Chapter 2, the managers of government services are required to operate them at the lowest cost. Sometimes however the managers of a state service can find themselves largely free of 'cost efficiency' supervision. Such a situation arose when the (British) Sudan Civil Service was formed in the 19th century. Hardly anyone knew what needed to be done in a remote and little known area. Consequently, when good men had been appointed to manage this Service, its organisation and subsequent operation (within its budget) was left largely in their hands. They naturally concentrated on getting the best people possible and on providing good conditions of service. That limited the numbers who could be employed: but it stimulated individuals by giving them wide responsibilities. It was easy thereafter for the Service to recruit only able and dedicated personnel.

The first result, as might be expected, was a very good Service for the Sudan. However the second (and possibly unexpected) result was a very cheap Service. The Sudan was governed at a fraction of the cost of what was normal

67

in either dictatorial or democratic conditions. In other words a state Service which was unusually free from supervision of its costs was unusually cost efficient. The people of the Sudan got better government at less cost, just because the government servants were left free to provide themselves with conditions which fulfilled them in their work.

The moral is that the best and cheapest service is provided by persons who feel fulfilled by their work. We have all seen some unit (say in a hospital) where the members take a pride in the service they give to the public, and which unit is thus highly cost efficient. This is not due to detailed supervision of the costs by higher authority. Rather the reverse, it is the result of local managers being free to provide their staff with conditions which make their work fulfilling. Esprit de corps is the key factor. Without it, soldiers run away in battle, policemen are dishonest and social workers are idle. Such behaviour is not cost efficient. The way to avoid it is to concentrate on providing the members of the Service with feelings of fulfilment, even though this may start by increasing costs.

It might be thought that this provides us with a model of the way in which people can obtain fulfilment in work which is controlled by their government. However the technique requires that the people concerned are persuaded to feel that they are doing something of importance for the community. They must regard themselves as somehow 'special': so that they take a pride in maintaining a high standard, and so that individuals who fail to do so are seen as letting the side down. This feeling is easy to induce in (say) a police force: but it would hardly be possible to persuade everybody at work that their particular form of production was somehow of special importance. It follows that this model is only capable of limited application.

Large Businesses

Although it is explained in Chapter 2 how the take-over bidder compels management to concentrate on profits for capitalist owners, there are exceptions. One is the family business. Such capitalists owners can, and sometimes do, operate their business primarily in the interests of its work force. This can produce as good a result as that provided by worker-ownership: but, unforunately, such an arrangement suffers from the fundamental defect of any benevolent dictatorship, which is that there is no known means of ensuring its perpetuation.

However, at the other end of the scale, there are very large enterprises which are too big for the normal take-over bidder. The managers of such businesses, being thus largely free from the constraints of capital ownership, can (if it suits them) operate the enterprises so as to give priority to the fulfilment of its employees. An example would seem to be provided by a firm called International Business Machines (IBM). A hierarchy of managers in IBM has the task of ensuring that every worker can express his views. Armed with this information, it is then the task of management to provide the workers with whatever seems most likely to fulfil them. This is of course precisely the same objective as that of the management of a worker-owned business.

It might be claimed that this is the objective of all enlightened managers nowadays: but that is not so. Let us take a practical example. The chief executive says to a departmental manager — "Our rivals are under cutting our price because they produce these components cheaper than we do. Why is your department (which produces these components) so inefficient?" The successful junior manager is the one who somehow reduces the costs, as quickly and as smoothly as possible. He may see that the measures he takes will reduce feelings of fulfilment in the workers and thus sow the seeds of future trouble: but, if he wants promotion, he will be wise to set aside such considerations .

IBM policy (it appears) is to do what the ordinary business manager cannot do, which is to give priority to the workers' interests. Thus the ordinary worker's greatest need is continuity of employment. Accordingly it is IBM policy to provide this, even when it may be necessary to close down an entire plant. The short term result is to increase costs: but in the long term it is claimed that IBM benefits. We thus observe the same effect as that in a comparable state service, which is that overall cost efficiency is increased by giving priority to the fulfilment of the workers.

It might thus be thought that all we have to do is to arrange for industrial managers to be freed from the take-over bidder, atleast in the short term. Then, provided that managers are made to understand this technique of saving money by spending it on workers fulfilment, both workers and capitalist business owners can attain their objectives in industry. Unfortunately this is not so.

Business Managers

The idea is that business managers should fulfil the lives of their workers and, in so doing, provide their capitalist masters with the most cost- efficient production. Unfortunately one of the ingredients of workers' fulfilment is a good financial reward for their work. This is of course one of the requirements which IBM provides. Indeed the ability to pay good wages arises, at least in part, from the cost efficiency of the work force. However it is in the nature of human endeavour that different business enterprises will achieve different financial results. Consequently, if all managerial teams adopt a policy of giving priority to workers' fulfilment, there will nevertheless be times in which some have to pay less than the average. Then those workers will be liable, indeed likely, to feel dissatisfied.

It often happens that a managerial team copes most efficiently with its business problems, but (for reasons beyond its control) temporarily makes less money than the current average. Unfortunately management is like justice. It must not only be good, but it must be seen to be good: and workers under control of capitalist managers will rarely feel satisfied when payed less than the average. It follows that control of work by managerial teams can only succeed in those enterprises which are currently doing at least as well as the average.

By contrast, a system of worker-ownership caters for all circumstances. If worker-owners feel less than satisfied, whether justifiably or not, the remedy lies in their own hands. Unhappiness springs from a situation in which a person is prevented from trying to improve his lot. People feel frustrated when they cannot get together in a joint effort to make their circumstances better. It is true that, when they are given this power, they may fail to improve anything: but that is a secondary consideration. It is the joint effort which provides their fulfilment.

Summary

Circumstances can arise in which the managers of a state service, or of a privately-owned business, give priority to the interests of those who work in the undertaking. In such circumstances the result can be an unusually high degree of cost effectiveness. It is thus arguable that both capital and labour can get what they want, provided the managers of an undertaking give priority to the fulfilment of labour.

Unfortunately this technique can only succeed a) in a state service when the work can be shown to be special in some way, and b) in a private business when the rewards available for the workers are currently at least as good as the average. By contrast, worker-ownership is able to provide fulfilment in all conditions.

PART II — PRACTICE

"Definition"

9 — Definition

"I believe this government cannot endure, half slave half free" — Abraham Lincoln

Synopsis

Industrial Democracy is the complement of political democracy.

Worker-Ownership is defined.

Need for Definition is explained.

Complications arise in practice.

Adulteration must be guarded against.

Co-operative Principles do not apply to worker-ownership.

Codification should be limited to the definition.

Industrial Democracy

The conclusion of the first part of this book is that there are enormous advantages in adopting a system of business ownership which will give us democratic control of our working lives. However we know that the practice of political democracy requires the maintenance of particular principles. These are well understood in the West, and we all instantly object if we see any infringement of (say) the secret ballot or a free Press. Unfortunately we do not yet realise that the practice of industrial democracy also requires the maintenance of certain essential principles, the infringement of which can be equally fatal to its practice. *

It is explained below (under 'Co-operative Principles') how it came about that the old Producer Co-operative movement failed to evolve any principles appropriate to its practice: and it is explained in Chapter 10 — History how that movement, after initial expansion, then declined and failed. In that chapter it is also explained how subsequent worker-ownership movements succeeded because, evolving the idea of industrial democracy afresh, they incorporated its essential principles into their practice. Hence the need to formulate a definition of worker-ownership, the maintenance of which will ensure its operation of industrial democracy

*Indeed, in the absence of any definition, it is difficult even to explain the practice of industrial democracy. It is as if we advocated political democracy without stating its essential principles, leaving enquirers to assume that any nation calling itself democratic must be demonstrating political democracy. The enquirers would soon become confused. Similarly, enquirers are confused if left to assume that any business calling itself a 'co-operative' is demonstrating the practice of industrial democracy.

There is another important reason for doing this. It is a rule of human endeavour that an undertaking will only succeed if all those concerned have, and maintain, an agreed objective. (That is why 'maintenance of the objective' is always taught as one of Principles of War.) However it is only possible to maintain an objective if we know precisely what that objective is. Industrial democracy is our aim: but we require to know the principles necessary for its operation.

The way to meet the above two requirements is to define a worker-owned business.

Worker-Ownership

A worker-owned business is owned (and therefore controlled) by those who supply it with it with labour instead of by those who supply it with capital. It is thus the exact opposite of a conventional business. That then is the way to define it. This is not at first easy to do, because we are so used to the conventional system of business ownership that we never think of defining it. However, on considering the matter, it is clear that a capital owned business is one in which —

1) ownership is exercised only by the suppliers of equity capital.

2) all these capitalists take part in the ownership.

3) the workers are rewarded by agreed wages and salaries.

4) the capitalists dispose of the variable income of the business.

If a worker-owned business is the precise opposite of the above, it follows that it is one in which -

1) ownership must be exercised only by the suppliers of labour.

2) all these workers must take part in the ownership.

3) the capitalists must be rewarded by agreed rates of interest.

4) the workers must dispose of the variable income of the business.

One other point is required, in order to deal with the fact that an individual can supply both labour and capital to a business. This is that —

5) the control and the benefits of the business must be divided between "the worker-owners in their capacity as suppliers of labour, and not in any capacity they may have as suppliers of capital. *

In the USA the Industrial Co-operative Association of Somerville Massachusetts holds that control of an industrial co-operative stems from the personal rights of the workers in it, rather than from their ownership of the

---

*In fact worker-owners nearly always become suppliers of capital because, if their enterprise is to succeed, they are bound to have to reinvest some of its earnings.

business assets. In this view the change is, not from capital ownership to worker-ownership, but from capital ownership to "democratic social institutions" controlled by members "with personal rights attached to the functional role of working in the enterprise". It is claimed that the workers are not owners of their business, because "any right attached to a person's functional role cannot be treated as a marketable property right". This leaves the enterprise apparently owned by no one, which (in this writer's view) is a *de facto* impossibility. In any event, the desired objective of control of work by people at work is achieved more simply by changing ownership from capitalists to workers.

As explained in the Introduction, it is perfectly possible to have some half-and-half arrangement in which ownership is shared between capital and labour. However the many advantages claimed for worker-ownership in the first part of this book are based on the assumption of a complete change-over from one form of ownership to the other. Hence the description of a worker-owned business as being one in which 'people acting in their capacity as suppliers of labour' enjoy all the rights and benefits normally accorded to 'people acting in their capacity as suppliers of capital'.

Reasons for Definition

When the concept of state ownership of industry was first put forward, no one doubted what was intended. This was the vesting of all the rights of ownership of an industry in the state: and, in so far as definition was required, that was how state ownership was defined. Similarly it might be assumed that the concept of worker-ownership must comprise the vesting of all the rights of ownership of a business in its workers, and that it would be so defined. However this is far from being what happens in practice.*

*The following are examples of divergent definitions:
a) One person, writing specifically about workers co-operatives, says that "co-operative legislation...is guided by the universally recognised principles of the International Co-operative Alliance: one member one vote: free and voluntary membership: limited remuneration of the under-written capital."
b) Another writer states that "the four criteria of a co-operative .. are ownership by the members, job rotation, consensus decision making by all the members and social as well as financial objectives."
a) Another writer states that "employee ownership will probably work best if it incorporates the following key features:
- the identity principle which enjoins that there should be an identity or near identity between those who are employed by a firm and those who own and control it.
- a requirement that all those employed by the employee owned firm must buy a significant parcel of shares in it.
- a bias towards allocating profits on the basis of 'patronage' rather than shareholding size.
- a restriction on share dealings between individual employees.
- a formula for buying out the shares of employees who leave, which is both fair to them and fair to those staying on."

There are people who already believe in the idea that work should be controlled by the persons who do the work, instead of by the persons who supply the money. Although these people may advocate the reform in order to achieve differing ends, they do all agree on the basic idea. That idea requires definition, firstly because it then becomes possible for those who share it to distinguish themselves from those who do not, and secondly (and perhaps more importantly) because it then becomes possible for observers to know what the idea is and to identify it in operation.

Complications

The need for precise definition arises from the complications which are liable to arise in practice, such as the following:-

- On the formation of a worker-owned business there is usually a problem of start-up capital. A capitalist may offer to supply the money in return for an equity share in the business. He may point out that interest has to be paid on a loan from the start, whereas equity shares need no servicing until the business is making a profit. He may even go so far as to agree to take no part in control. This is where a firm definition prevents prospective worker-owners from making a mistake which can never afterwards be remedied. To accept (any substantial amount of) equity capital is for worker-owners to sell their birthright. All future members of that business will suffer a reduction in one of the main advantages of worker-ownership, which is the ability of workers to use their own labour to enhance their own earnings (in either cash or capital) . This is the kind of adulteration of genuine worker-ownership which resulted in the failure of the British producer co-operative movement.

- A situation can arise in which the only people available with a particular skill comprise individuals, who will come and work for a wage but who (at first) refuse to become owner members. A small infraction of a rule of definition is obviously not of importance, and a few non-members in a business will not invalidate the operation of worker-ownership. However there is a danger that any infraction may become the thin end of a wedge. Thus in 1970 the French producer co-operative organisation (SCOP) had about 30,000 workers, of whom some 15,000 were not members of their co-operatives. Therefore, if any non-members are allowed in a worker-owned business, it should be laid down that they must not exceed (say) 5% of the total membership.

- Another complication arises if members wish to have some scheme which gives them personal capital holdings in their business. A definition requires to make it clear that they must not thus obtain benefit in their capacity as suppliers of capital. The Mondragon organisers saw this danger when they formulated their 'capital credits' scheme. They thus

76

arranged that individual credits should be treated as loan capital, to be requited only with rates of fixed interest.

- However the members of some worker-owned business may prefer to acquire shares in their business, which will appreciate (or not) in accordance with their conduct of the enterprise. It is possible to do this, and to maintain the definition, if issues of shares are always either equal for all or in accordance with members' job ratings. In this way any benefit accruing to a holder of shares will always be in accordance with the work which that member has supplied.*

- A question arises as to whether the members of a worker-owned businesses should enjoy their rights equally or in accordance with their job ratings. There are two tenable theories. One is that, since the members normally work for the same hours each day, they provide an equal amount of work. The other is that the amount of their work varies according to their skill. The originators of the Mondragon organisation started by having both voting rights and the business earnings allocated on the same basis, which was that of job ratings: but after three years they decided to change the former to one-man-one-vote. This is the universal voting procedure in worker-owned businesses, although the members usually divide their earnings on the basis of job ratings. The custom of one-man-one-vote stems from political democracy (where there is no means of determining the relative merits of different citizens) rather than from any logical thinking about industrial democracy.

Adulteration

A definition of a worker-owned business should provide a simple framework, outside which genuine worker-ownership is not recognised, but inside which everything is subject to trial and error. Failing such definition, adulteration is likely in two ways.

Firstly, different people have their own ideas of which practices are essential to the success of worker-ownership, and they are liable to try to include these in its definition. However, whilst the definition of worker-ownership is a matter of logic, the best ways of making it work are a matter of

*In Britain in 1983, workers in the newly-formed National Freight Corporation were encouraged to buy shares in it, as a result of which the enterprise became substantially worker owned. This was a good way of spreading ownership of industry amongst the citizens of Britain. However it was not the worker-ownership described in this book, because the rights of ownership were distributed according to the capital, and not the labour, which individuals supplied. It is true that many of the workers have thus been motivated to support their business: but they will fail to obtain most of the advantages described in this book. Further, when in due course they are able to sell their shares on the open market, a process will be started which disperses these among the general public: so that, eventually, the enterprise will become a conventional capital-owned undertaking — unless of course the workers concerned read this book and demand a re-arrangement of the ownership of the business which will provide them with the real thing!

77

trial and error. Some of us may think we know what is essential to success: but we must not be allowed to prevent others from experimenting. *

Secondly, people often espouse worker-ownership in order to bring about particular ethical or social reforms. Hence they are liable to represent these further aims as a necessary part of worker-ownership. However it is not our purpose to free people from control by capital in order to impose any other form of control on them. We can all unite in seeking to free people at work: but it is hard enough persuading people of the need for this, without making the task more difficult by additional requirements.†

Co-operative Principles

Much confusion arises from the custom of referring to businesses which are owned by their workers as co-operatives, because this leads people to assume that such enterprises must conform to co-operative principles.

The Rochdale Pioneers founded both the 'consumer' and 'producer' co-operative movements, the former to benefit consumers and the latter to benefit producers. However, since the consumer movement expanded much faster than the producer movement, attention was at first concentrated on the former. The success of consumer co-operation soon attracted people who wished to join the band wagon for their own advantage. Some of these then initiated consumer co-operatives in which entrance fees had to be paid to the original members (themselves) by those joining afterwards: whilst others arranged for high rates of interest to be paid on the capital with which they initiated the co-operatives. The wise founders of the consumer movement saw that these practices diverted it from its objective. Accordingly they enunciated the principles of 'free entry' and 'a limited return on capital'. Further principles of operation were established as other problems arose.

Unfortunately, because consumer co-operation was so widely successful, people unthinkingly applied its principles to the practice of producer co-operation, forgetting that the latter had (and has) a different objective. This

*For example, when the British government defined a "co-operative or common ownership", one of the "points included was a proviso that such a business could not be sold by its members for their personal gain. This was to guard against what had happened in the past, when successful co-operatives had been sold to enable the members to get control of the capital assets which they had built up: but, although such a proviso might be a desirable operating rule, it reduces rather than enhances ownership by workers. It is thus illogical to include it as part of the definition of worker-ownership. It further transpires that such a rule is unnecessary when an enterprise has some form of personal capital holdings scheme.

†Christianity is a case in point. It is reasonable to wish to include its principles in any reform of industry. However no reform at all will take place until people can be freely persuaded to adopt it, and many of them will dislike the imposition of any religious ideas. The only objective on which all will agree is that of freedom. It follows that the Christian must first offer people at work freedom to do what they like. Then, when they have attained the freedom of worker-ownership, he can endeavour to persuade them to use it in the cause of Christianity.

78

mistake is apparent from the two examples of co-operative principles noted above:

a) Free entry to a consumer co-operative is important because the more members it can get, the more it prospers. A producer co-operative (which is to say a worker-owned business) has, by contrast, to restrict membership on a number of grounds. Free entry can be interpreted to mean freedom from any bar to entry on grounds of race, religion or colour: but the point is of doubtful validity.*

b) A limited return on capital is always desirable: but there is no danger of producer co-operative members paying more for their capital than the lowest available rate. The important principle to which they must adhere is that their capital must only be borrowed.

Whatever may be thought about the evolution of co-operative principles, the important point is that their application to producer co-operation resulted in the failure of that movement to establish any principles of its own. This was a major cause of its adulteration and eventual failure. Hence the urgency now of establishing a definition of worker-ownership which will prevent it too from becoming adulterated.

Codification

The definition of a worker-owned business should be codified, and preferably by law. However any legal codification of worker-ownership practice, within that definition, is a mistake. This was something learned to its cost by the French producer co-operative movement (SCOP).

In the 19th century Napoleon III wished to assist the comparatively new French producer co-operative movement: and one of the things he did was to codify its practice under French law. Unfortunately this proved to be a serious handicap later, because a parliamentary democracy always has difficulty in finding time to alter laws which affect only a small number of its citizens. The French movement was thus prevented from progressing for a long time thereafter.

It follows that, whilst it is important to have a clear logical definition of worker-ownership, nothing should be done to inhibit its evolution by trial and error within that definition. This does not prevent particular associations of worker-owned enterprises from formulating their own rules of operation, because people who join the group do so of their own free will. However it is desirable to have more than one such group so that there is a practical choice. A potential weakness of the Mondragon group is that Basques who wish to

---

*Thus no one objected to the establishment in London of a workers co-operative bakery operated only by West Indians.

become worker-owners have no practical alternative to accepting the particular methods of operation evolved by that group.*

Summary

A definition of worker-ownership is necessary, firstly in order to establish the principles without which industrial democracy lacks reality, and secondly in order to ensure that all concerned have (and maintain) a clear objective. Since worker-ownership is the opposite of capital ownership, it should be so defined. That is a matter of logic, whereas the ways in which worker-ownership is best operated are a matter for trial and error. Precise definition of worker-ownership is required, because of the complications liable to arise in its practice and the danger that it will become adulterated like the old producer co-operative movement. This definition should be codified, preferably by law: but the operation of worker-ownership, within its definition, should be free for individual experiment.

*Although (as recorded in Chapter 13) one enterprise has recently seceded from the group because of disagreement with its rules.

"History is Bunk" — Henry Ford

10 — History

"What we learn from history is that we do not learn from history" — G. W. F. Hegel

Synopsis

The Rochdale Pioneers started both 'consumer and 'producer' co-operation'.

Eastern Europe provided fertile ground at the end of the second world war.

Genuine Industrial Democracy is operated in Eastern Europe.

Importance of East Europe lies in its confirmation of Mondragon practice.

Mondragon provided similar fertile ground a decade later.

Yugoslavia operates a special Self Management system.

Recent Initiatives in worker-ownership are now taking place in the West.

The Rochdale Pioneers

The idea of worker-ownership goes back to Robert Owen in Scotland and people like Philippe Buchez in France: but its main initiation was by the Rochdale Pioneers, who started both the 'consumer' and the 'producer' co-operative movements. Although the practice of consumer co-operation spread much faster, producer co-operatives were also set up in most countries of the world. However, after a period, the producer movement began to decline: so that, except in France and Italy, it had largely ceased to exist by the end of the second world war.

It is not always realised that consumer and producer co-operation are two very different concepts. The former deals with the comparatively limited problem of the distribution of goods, whilst the latter embraces all aspects of work. In the changed conditions brought about by the factory age, ordinary people suffered both as consumers and as workers. In order to remedy this the Rochdale Pioneers initiated two movements, both of which required people to 'cooperate' with one another in appropriate business undertakings. However arrangements for consumers to control distribution have only a limited relation to arrangements for workers to control work. Indeed the point is often overlooked that the work in a consumer co-operative is not controlled by its workers.

Although consumer co-operatives soon became a large success — until overtaken by the chain stores — the spread of producer co-operatives was much slower. This was mainly because it was easier to start a consumer owned retail shop than a producer owned business. Being thus overshadowed by the consumer movement, the producer co-operative movement mistakenly adopted consumer co-operative 'principles'. Lacking principles of its own, it then became adulterated and, after initial expansion, gradually ran down. Although the movement virtually ceased to exist in Britain, it continued in France and Italy. Even there however (and subject to recent developments by SCOP in France) the movement has failed to attract many ordinary workers.

Producer Co-operation

Some people ascribe the failure of producer co-operatives to a hostile environment: but the environment was (and is) merely neutral. Although it is always difficult to establish new ways of doing things, there were 100,000 members of producer co-operatives in Britain in 1900: and these were quite sufficient to demonstrate a new industrial technique. If therefore that technique did not spread it can only have been due to its being found unattractive by ordinary workers.

There have been some large and successful producer co-operatives: but their failure to attract imitators may be gauged from the following examples —

- A plywood manufacturing enterprise on the Western side of America was so successful that its members sold it in order to benefit from the capital assets they had created in the business. Had producer co-operation evolved any personal capital holdings schemes, this would have been unnecessary and others might then have copied the plywood business.
- A French producer co-operative was extremely successful in the 1970s: but it consisted of 100 members with some 900 ordinary non-member workers, whose position was little different from that of a worker in a conventional business. Such arrangements obviously failed to appeal to others.
- A successful British worker-owned chemical company (Scott Bader) with over 400 members operates on the basis of devoting its profits to social purposes. However, although this may be a worthy objective, it is not one likely to attract ordinary workers. Nor has it.

Eastern Europe

In the hard times in Eastern Europe which followed the end of the second world war, many people started worker-owned enterprises (which they called 'workers co-operatives'), as being the only form of free enterprise permitted by their new masters. However, since communist economic theory assumed state ownership of all the means of production, they were given little (if any) encouragement. They were seen as small collections of artisans, which would be phased out of the economy when state ownership was fully established. They were thus largely ignored, whilst officials got on with organising the basic industries.

The result was to channel the practice of worker-ownership into the small business sector of the economies of the five countries concerned: and, when the planners in each country got around to this sector, they found most of it already being operated by workers' co-operatives. They further found that these co-operatives provided all their own capital and served the public in this sector better than state enterprises. This conclusion was not reached without some friction, such as the 'nationalisation' of a number of successful food manufacturing co-operatives in Poland. However in 1968 the Hungarian government, which had given its workers' co-operatives no assistance at all up to that point, decided to accept them as a permanent part of its economy. This signified a general change of view in all the countries concerned.

Since about 1970 there have thus been more than a million worker-owners in Poland, Czechoslovakia, Hungary, Romania and Bulgaria. (The practice was not allowed in Russia itself nor in East Germany.) The movements are no longer expanding because of their political confinement to the small business sector. Their rapid initial expansion, and their ability to accumulate large group capital funds, was largely due to the absence of conventional (capital owned) businesses. The main lessons to be learned from their operation stem from the time when their countries' economies were still in a state of flux and commercial efficiency was essential to the success of the new enterprises.

Actual numbers of people engaged are 1,300,000 in Hungary, 500,000 in Poland, 300,000 in Romania, 175,000 in Czechoslovakia, (no figures for Bulgaria). The very big figure in Hungary is accounted for by the fact that over 70% of Hungarian agriculture is operated by workers co-operatives, which alone have a million members.* Considering only industrial co-operatives, Poland† and Hungary have the most members per head of population.

Genuine Democracy

Western observers have become so accustomed to misuse of the word 'democratic' in Eastern Europe that they tend to discount the possibility of any form of real democracy there. Surprisingly however, these workers co-operatives really are worker-owned. Their practice of industrial democracy, in all the countries concerned, is limited in only three ways —

- They must confine themselves to the small business sector. They cannot expand worker-ownership into any of the main industries.
- The co-operatives must conform to state economic planning. Thus (for example) they cannot provide services not wanted by the state.

*Agricultural co-operatives exist outside Hungary: but these are no more than associations of capital owned undertakings which pool their selling and buying arrangements.
†It is of interest that over half of the Polish workers co-operative members are women.

- There must be no suggestion whatever of industrial democratic practice being extended into the political sphere.

Beyond the three points set out above, the co-operatives can do what they like. State officials are happy to be relieved of the problems of running a difficult sector of industry. The members thus elect their own business directors at enterprise, group and national headquarters level. It is unlikely that the Russians approve of this: but it is not worth their while making an issue of something that only affects 10% of their satellite's industries.

The fact that these democratic arrangements are genuine can be checked by personal observation. Since the Poles pull no punches in criticising their government, the facts about their workers' co-operatives are readily discussed: and the truth is not difficult to ascertain elsewhere by anyone making personal enquiry. The picture which emerges is one of genuine democratic control, with full freedom of discussion and elections by secret vote on a one-man-one-vote basis.

The East European enterprises all work together in groups, with elected group directors who in turn elect directors to their national headquarters. Most of these groups are on a territorial basis, coinciding with government local authority areas. However there are a few groups in Poland which are formed on a trade basis and cover the whole country.

Importance

The importance of these East European worker-ownership movements lies in their confirmation of Mondragon practice. They evolved before Mondragon: but, since there was no communication with Spain under Franco, the Mondragon organisers did not even know of their existence. Nevertheless the methods of operating worker-ownership in Mondragon are remarkably similar to those in Eastern Europe. This is despite the fact that the Mondragon enterprises had to compete with conventional capital owned businesses, whereas those in East Europe did not.

The most obvious similarity between the movements in Mondragon and Eastern Europe is their adherence to 'pure' worker-ownership, which is to say a complete reversal of the roles of capital and labour. This means that ownership of a business is confined to those working in it, that all (or virtually all) the workers take part in ownership, and that the rights and benefits of ownership are enjoyed by the workers in relation to the labour (and not to any capital) they supply.* All other arrangements are subject to trial and error, although it is remarkable how similarly these have evolved in the organisations concerned.

*This is achieved in practice by having one-man-one-vote.

Mondragon

Since quite a number of reports have been published on the Mondragon organisation, comment here is limited to those points which are not stressed elsewhere.

Firstly, the Mondragon bank tends to be seen as a vital part of the organisation. This is misleading. The savings bank, which borrows money from the public and lends it to the enterprises, is undoubtedly useful: but you can borrow money without owning a bank. The key factor has been the Management Division of the bank, which acts as the headquarters of the enterprises. Indeed this division is now being separated from the bank and set up on its own. Its most important work has been its evolution of techniques which ensure that borrowed capital is always repaid.

Secondly, the formation and success of the Ularco combination* of enterprises and the subsequent getting together of most of the Mondragon co-operatives in Ularco type combines was an important development. It shows how worker-owned businesses can do what is not possible for enterprises in capital ownership, which is to gain all the advantages of conventional business combines without sacrificing individual ownership and control (see 'Business Combines' in Chapter 13 — Grouping).

Thirdly, the logical originators of the Mondragon organisation took care to avoid use of the word 'wages'. They substituted the word *'anticipos'*, meaning a distribution of money in advance of the business earnings. The importance of this is dealt with in Appendix K.

Fourthly, the Mondragon enterprises did not start as co-operatives. They were simply enterprises owned by their workers. However, when it was desired to start a savings bank, Father Arizmendi discovered that this could be done under existing Spanish co-operative law. Accordingly the enterprises and their new bank registered themselves as co-operatives. Even so, when some of the old producer co-operatives in the area wished to join the Mondragon organisation, they were rejected on the grounds that they had a lot of non-member workers and that this did not accord with the Mondragon definition of a business owned by its workers.

Fifthly, the operation of their own health and social security services by the Mondragon group members shows how the state can decentralise these to great advantage.

Groups

In both Mondragon and Eastern Europe it can be seen that worker-owned enterprises all operate in federal groups, with the addition of the closer grouping of most of the enterprises of the Mondragon group into various

*The name Ularco has since been changed to Fagor, which is the brand name of the goods produced.

smaller 'combines'. As explained in the second point under 'Mondragon' above, this phenomenon demonsrates the ability of worker-owned enterprises to work very closely together whilst retaining separate identity. Thus the member enterprises delegate control to their group or combine headquarters only to the extent that all agree: and, should an enterprise disagree seriously with the policy of itgs group, it always has the right to secede.

The reason for the ability of worker-owned enterprises to behave like this is that they do not compete with each other for sales, as explained in Chapter 5.* As appears further on in this book, this is a most important factor in the operation of worker-ownership. Unfortunately its practice is only so far observable in Mondragon and Eastern Europe, where there are enough worker-owned enterprises to take advantage of it.

Yugoslavia

The Self Management system in Yugoslavia is not of direct interest, because it is an arrangement in which the rights of ownership are shared between the workers in a business and their local authority. Nevertheless it is worthy of study, because it has given the Yugoslavs much experience of the problems of industrial democracy. The evidence is that, although the Self Management system is state policy, it is in fact freely accepted by the people. What nobody knows, including the Yugoslavs themselves, is how the people would react if the alternatives of either conventional capital ownership or full worker-ownership were made available.

The Recent Initiatives

In the last decade or so, that is since about 1970, there has been a resurgence of interest in the idea of 'control of work by people at work': and new organisations in various countries of the West have been formed to promote its practice. There has also been some expansion of the old producer co-operative organisations in France and Italy. However, although there are individually successful enterprises (such as Scott Bader in England), there is as yet no demonstration of the general success of a number of enterprises all operating in the same way. Nor is there much evidence that any of the new initiatives are attracting ordinary workers.

This is not to deny that much has been discovered (or rediscovered) by the thousands of people taking part in these new initiatives. The enquirer can thus learn a great deal from them. What they do not demonstrate however is any firm evidence of success in promoting a way of work with wide appeal. This is perhaps an unkind comment on an organisation such as SCOP in France, which has continued in existence since the days of Napoleon III,

*And, should any readers have doubted that theory, here is the evidence of its working in practice.

which has a dedicated central staff, and which has modified its rules and achieved substantial expansion in the last decade. Nevertheless there is as yet no evidence that it appeals to more than a limited selection of French workers.

Summary

The practice of both consumer and producer co-operation was taken up all over the world: but, whereas the former was widely successful (until overtaken by the chain stores), the latter expanded more slowly and then went into a decline, until only the French and Italian movements remained. This was because of its failure to evolve principles to maintain its objective of industrial democracy.

New worker-ownership movements evolved after the second world war, firstly in Eastern Europe and then in the Basque province of Spain, which have achieved large success. They demonstrate the need to adhere to a logical definition of worker-ownership: and they provide a blue-print of the practices which succeed, especially that of grouping.

A recent widespread resurgence in the West of attempts at control of work by people at work does not yet demonstrate anything definite.

"Finance"

11 — Finance

"Attempt the end and never stand to doubt. Nothing's so hard
but search will find it out" — Richard Lovelace

Synopsis

Risk Labour replaces risk capital.

Hire Purchase is the principle on which this is done.

Group Finance is the necessary means.

Start-Up Conditions are explained.

Workers Commitment to their enterprises is essential.

Commercial Viability is necessary but is different.

Advice and Aid by the lenders is essential.

Evolution of this technique is described.

Liquidation of worker-owned enterprises should be abnormal.

State Finance is unnecessary and anyhow impractical.

Conclusions are drawn.

Risk Labour

Adam Smith explained how 'the wealth of nations' lies primarily in the work capacity of their citizens. Hence the fact that most of the capital used by industry is that which industry itself creates. Worker-owned businesses are no exception: but they have a problem at the start, because workers will often have no capital of their own, and because they cannot accept 'equity' investment which would entitle non-workers to a share in their profits.*

The problem is thus how worker-owners can substitute risk labour for risk capital, particularly in borrowing money to start a new business. It is important to understand that this problem has been solved and that the solution can be examined in practical operation.

Hire Purchase

The principle on which worker-owners can acquire start-up capital is that of hire-purchase.† The widespread use of hire purchase evolved after the first

*Or which would result in the earnings of the business being distributed to its workers according to the capital, instead of the labour, they supply.

†Since it has become customary to offer almost all goods (and many services) on deferred payment terms, the phrase 'hire purchase' is now seldom used. It was coined in the past to describe the then novel technique of giving immediate delivery of goods with an agreement for deferred payment.

world war, when observers at first regarded it as a very risky practice. However it soon became apparent that, if people had the means of payment, they rarely defaulted on HP agreements: and it was this discovery which led to the great spread of HP sales in the inter-war years. In the 1930s, the directors of one of the big musical companies in Britain were advised to offer their customers HP facilities. With some reluctance, the directors formed a subsidiary company to carry out this 'money lending' operation. They were amazed to find, at the end of the first year, that the subsidiary company had made a bigger profit than the parent manufacturing company.

Since it is now well established that (in the appropriate conditions) you can safely lend one man the money with which to buy a washing machine, it is logical to assume that (in the appropriate conditions) you can equally well lend one hundred men the money with which to buy a factory. This idea may seem to be at variance with the record of workers' co-operatives as borrowers: but that is because no hire-purchase technique was applied in the past. Someone who simply lends money to people can expect to lose much of it. The same thing is likely to happen to persons (or governments) who simply make loans to workers cooperatives.

Group Finance

It has been shown how worker-owned enterprises naturally get together in (local or trade) groups. This enables money to be borrowed from normal sources of finance by the group, against both the assets of the established enterprises and the record of the group as a borrower. Since these are factors well understood by normal sources of finance, an established group of worker-owned businesses has no problem in getting all the money it wishes to borrow. The hire-purchase operation only starts when the money is on-lent within the group. This is the task of the headquarters staff of the group.

The reader will ask "but what is done when there are too few worker-owned enterprises to form an appropriate group?" The answer is that this is the initial hump which the promotion of worker-ownership has to surmount. Obviously some risk capital, necessarily provided by some philanthropic means, is required in the early stages of the promotion of worker-ownership. The problem is considered in detail in Chapter 15. Meanwhile it is important to understand that 'revolving loan funds' are only a temporary answer to the problem of worker-ownership finance. These are useful only in order to establish the groups of worker-owned businesses, which will be able to borrow whatever capital is required and which will evolve the hire-purchase technique of lending to their member enterprises with security of repayment.

Start-Up Conditions

The technique of hire-purchase requires, firstly that the borrower shall enter into a firm commitment to repay, and secondly that he shall have the means of so doing. Both these conditions apply to the provision of start-up capital for worker-owned businesses within a group: but the second condition involves the lender (the group headquarters), not just in examining the circumstances of the borrower, but in actively assisting the borrower to service and repay the loan. The criteria for lending may thus be divided into three, of which the last is the most difficult to arrange —

1) The business which borrows must be so organised as to commit its members to its (eventual) success.
2) The venture for which the money is borrowed must be (as far as can be ascertained) commercially viable.
3) The lenders must be able to provide the borrowers with continuing advice and aid.

Workers Commitment

As explained, the exponents of hire-purchase discovered that people who enter into a firm commitment to repay a loan will normally do so if they have the means. A group headquarters staff thus has first to satisfy itself that the members of the enterprises to which they lend money do feel themselves so committed. This in turn means that those enterprises are organised in such a way as to ensure that their members intend to stick to them.

Once a worker-owned business is in operation, the continuing determination of its members to keep it in being (and therefore to honour its commitments) depends mainly on the way it has been set up and organised. Many of the arrangements in Chapter 13 are recommended with this in mind, whilst Chapter 14 deals specifically with the subject of Motivation. However the final decision on the way in which this HP requirement shall be implemented must rest with the lenders, i.e. the elected directors of the headquarters of each group.

Commercial Viability

Obviously loans must be confined to ventures which appear likely to succeed. However the dangers of failure are much less for worker-owned enterprises than for conventional ones.

Firstly, there is the large amount of money which members are able* to save by reduced cash drawings in the early days of an enterprise or when times are difficult.* If it is argued that workers would never make such sacrifices, it must be remembered that workers on strike often make much bigger sacrifices when they expect long-term benefit as a result. Further, it is quite normal for people to forego a substantial proportion of their income in order to hire purchase particular goods. It is reasonable to suppose that people might

---

*The amount potentially available will not mormally be less than the difference between unemployment pay and normal wages.

make the same kind of sacrifices to acquire their own business as to acquire their own home.

Secondly, although the failure rate of new enterprises in conventional ownership is very high, it is much lower when such enterprises are set up by business combines. The central staff of a group of worker-owned enterprises is normally both larger and more concerned to keep its member enterprises in being, than is the comparable staff of a conventional business combine. There is also the point that all concerned in a worker-owned group will help a member enterprise if they can.

Thirdly, worker-owners differ from capitalist business owners (as already explained) in giving security of work priority over maximisation of earnings. When this policy is permanently pursued by a group of businesses, it makes a greater difference to what happens than might be thought. For example, much more attention is paid to planning for variations in production or sales in advance of their possible need.

Notwithstanding the above, group staffs obviously take the greatest care to examine commercial prospects before making loans to start new enterprises. The point is that, if mistakes are made, the margin for error is so large that recovery is (in Mondragon experience) virtually always possible.

Advice and Aid

A group headquarters staff must not only check the viability of each loan, but they must actively assist in its success. Hence the need for an arrangement whereby worker-owners (in effect) lend to themselves. The most common causes of the failure of new businesses are insufficient market research, poor financial control and bad management.* Thereafter help is required in such matters as technical research and long-term market planning, for which the managers of a small business rarely have the time or the facilities. Details of all the ways in which a group central staff deals with these problems form the main subject of Chapter 13.

Evolution

It is interesting to see how the technique of group borrowing and internal distribution of loan finance was evolved in two of the successful worker-ownership organisations.

In Mondragon, the original idea was that workers would provide their own capital. However the need for loan finance soon arose: and hence the formation of the savings bank. It was obvious to all concerned that this bank

---

*Great care is taken by the Mondragon group staff to try and launch a new business with an able manager. Nevertheless it is recounted that one enterprise required two changes of manager in its first year of operation.

would fail if its depositors ever lost their money. At the same time unemployment was so high that the members of a Mondragon enterprise were strongly motivated to maintain it. In consequence, during the first ten years or so, large sacrifices were often made to ensure that all the enterprises were kept afloat and able to service their bank loans.

By the early 1970s two changes had taken place. Firstly the management division of the bank had got going, and secondly affluence had made the members of the Mondragon enterprises less likely to accept large sacrifices of earnings. The result was the evolution of loan conditions by the members of the management division, which enabled them to avoid ever starting a new business which failed to survive and service its loan capital. What the management division had in fact done was to learn how to apply hire-purchase technique to the finance of worker-ownership.*

In Poland, some government finance had been made available to the workers' co-operatives from the start: and some of this money was lost through enterprise failures. However (as already explained) the absence of conventional businesses resulted in conditions which made it comparatively easy for the co-operatives to 'make money'. At the same time they were keen to avoid dependence on government finance. Hence the building up of large reserve funds at group and national level.† However the members of the Polish co-operatives were no more anxious to lose the money they had saved than were the depositors in the Mondragon savings bank. Hence the gradual evolution of the same technique of having large staffs at group (or the central union) headquarters, which had to discover how to loan money without losing it. This was easier in the East European economy, firstly because co-operative members could not get well paid jobs in private industry if they abandoned their enterprises, and secondly because control of wages and prices enabled the government to avoid any general business recessions (see Chapter 4).

---

*This picture is perhaps over-simplified. When asked how they can be sure of keeping every enterprise in being and able to repay its borrowing, the members of the management team are inclined to shake their heads and deny that they give any such guarantee. Nevertheless they have weathered a world recession without their policy breaking down. None of the Mondragon members has been required to live on less than 80% of local wage rates, no appreciable losses have been made on loans, and the policy of each enterprise being responsible for its own affairs has been largely maintained — much assisted by the enterprises operating in local or trade combines.

†The leaders of the Polish workers co-operative organisation did consider the idea of starting a bank: but this would have required the establishment of branches all over Poland. When techniques had been evolved for lending money from co-operative funds without serious risk of loss, it was found simpler for the staffs at group (or national) headquarters to guarantee loans made directly to co-operatives by local banks. The staffs made the same judgements and gave the same assistance as was found necessary in making loans from co-operative funds. The Mondragon enterprises could equally well borrow from local banks: but their savings bank is so efficiently operated that it is able to loan money at much below equivalent Spanish market rates.

Liquidation

We are so used to the liquidation of conventional businesses, that we assume that the ability of the Mondragon group to keep its enterprises in being must be the result of some exceptional circumstances. However the only exceptional circumstance is that the enterprises are worker-owned.

The failure and liquidation of business enterprises is primarily a phenomenon of the capital ownership system, in which minimum wage rates are essential. A conventional business enterprise is burdened, firstly with the need to maximise earnings (on comparatively short term), and secondly with the need to pay fixed wages and salaries.* As explained in Chapter 4, this leaves a comparatively small margin for profits, with the danger of liquidation if this margin disappears. An entirely different situation arises when businesses are operated for the long term security of their owners, who can make large variations in the amount of the money they draw out (and can also vary the amount of the work they supply).

It may be thought that bodies of worker-owners will be less ready to make sacrifices in order to maintain their businesses than are individuals who keep up HP payments in order to maintain ownership of personal goods. However the main problem of HP loans to individuals is the occasional maverick who defaults. This danger disappears when loans are made to bodies of worker-owners, because unreliable individuals have to submit to the majority.

State Finance

Some people think that worker-ownership should be financed by the state. However this is either unnecessary or impossible. It is unnecessary when, as has been shown above, groups of worker-owned businesses can get all the money they need from normal sources of finance. If however it is intended that state finance should take risks which are unacceptable to normal sources of finance, then the idea is impossible. No democratic state is able to finance any substantial proportion of its industry on a continued loss making basis.

State finance of worker-ownership is thus only a practical idea if limited in extent or time. There is indeed a case for state assistance in establishing the groups of worker-owned businesses necessary to operate the hire-purchase technique: but, lacking dictatorial powers, that is about as far as any Western government can be expected to go.

Conclusions and Summary

The key to the finance of worker-ownership is a hire purchase technique operated within each group of enterprises, which borrow capital from normal sources of finance against the security of the group as a whole. This capital is

*It is true that worker-owners will have a commitment to pay interest on borrowed capital: but this will normally be very much less of a burden than the need always to pay minimum wages.

96

on-lent to existing or new enterprises within the group, in such circumstances as are deemed to give it complete security.

Each worker-ownership group must therefore have a central staff capable, firstly of ensuring (the usual HP conditions) that the borrowers are capable of repayment and that they feel committed to do so, and secondly of providing the borrowers with continuing advice and aid.

"Workers Control"

12 — Operation

"It is always a silly thing to give advice, but to give good advice is absolutely fatal" — Oscar Wilde

Synopsis

Objectives of a worker-owned business must be agreed.

Membership conditions are explained.

Principles are those of the definition.

Democratic Control arrangements are explained.

Cash Distribution arrangements are explained.

Entrance Fees are necessary.

Capital Holdings are explained.

Legal Rules are explained.

Objectives

A human enterprise which fails to progress towards agreed goals will inevitably regress to eventual dissolution. As explained in Chapter 3, the object of capital ownership is production for money, and the system ensures that business managers pursue this object. Worker-owners by contrast can have complex objectives. Consequently it is important for the members of a worker-owned business to know, and to agree, what they want to achieve. At first this may be no more than a livelihood: but, even when that is the immediate objective, people usually have some idea what further goals they have in mind. They may just want more money: but, whatever their ideas may be, these should be shared. Then the members can become 'a band of brothers' united in joint endeavour. It is particularly important that the managers who lead them should share their aims.

Membership

Since the members of a worker-owned business have to agree their objectives, it is desirable for them to be like-minded people. For example, they may all want to get rich or they may all enjoy a particular form of production or they may all belong to the same ethnic group — or they may just be people who have got used to working together. It helps if the product of a worker-owned business is something prestigious. One point is widely agreed, which is that prospective new members should do a period of (say) six months working in the business, before taking up membership. This allows the

99

individual to discover whether he or she likes the other members and vice versa.

Principles

The essential principles to which the business must adhere are contained in the definition of worker-ownership. Other rules may be thought important, for example an entrance fee and individual capital holdings: but care should be taken by the members not to impose rules upon themselves which cannot easily be altered by themselves. No one can say in advance what new situations may arise or what new ideas may emerge. Of course it may be desired to join a group of worker-owned businesses, which requires its member enterprises to conform to its own detailed rules of operation. In such circumstances a right to secede should be retained.

Democratic Control

It is considered in Mondragon that industrial democracy begins to be difficult to operate if the members in a business exceed 400. One Polish writer has also named that figure. The Hungarians prefer numbers not to exceed 200. The important point to remember is that all the advantages of scale can be obtained by small worker-owned enterprises working together in 'Ularco' type combines (see 'Mondragon' in Chapter 10). In most circumstances, therefore, there is no object in increasing the size of a worker-owned business beyond (say) 200.

Since the objectives of worker-owners can be complex, they need to exercise more detailed control of their enterprise than do conventional business owners. However it would not be possible for all the members of an enterprise to have the detailed discussions with the managers necessary to consider their advice and to judge their competence. Hence the technique explained below of elected directors, who appoint and direct the management. It might be thought that such an arrangement would lead to friction between elected directors and professional managers. However the authority of the directors derives from their election, whilst that of the managers derives from their executive ability. The latter is necessarily subordinate to the former: but the two spheres are, or can be, distinct.

Where there are only a dozen or so members of an enterprise they can meet together at will. In such circumstances, formalities are hardly necessary. Consequently the arrangements set out below envisage an enterprise of at least (say) 25 people —

The General Assembly of the members is the sovereign body of the enterprise. It meets, under an elected chairman, as often as may be agreed. Its members will normally have one vote each: and there should be a provision for secret voting if required. If the enterprise joins in a combine, the General Assemblies of the enterprises concerned must delegate agreed powers to a central combine Assembly.

The Directing Committee is elected by the General Assembly to direct the enterprise in accordance with Assembly policies. The number of Committee members will normally be between 7 and 13. Their periods of office should not be less than a year. The Committee appoints and directs —

The Management Board, which can conveniently comprise 1 or 3 or 5 persons. Professional managers will normally expect a contract of service. They should always be, or become, members of the enterprise.

When an enterprise exceeds (say) 50 members, frequent General Assembly meetings become impractical. Experience has shown that effective democratic control requires some arrangement for worker-owners to be able to express their views whenever problems arise. Hence —

A Works Council is elected by the General Assembly on a 'shop' basis.* The Council members have no powers: but they have access to the directors and management. Their task is to oil the wheels of democracy by telling the leaders what is currently thought by the members 'on the shop floor', and vica versa.

A Supervisory Committee, probably comprising 3 persons, is desirable to check-up on the leaders on behalf of the members. This Committee would (for example) examine managerial expense accounts.

Cash Distribution

As explained in Appendix K, wages (in the normal meaning of the term) cannot exist in a worker-owned business. The members simply draw their own money out of the business and divide it amongst themselves. They must take (each week or each month) enough to support themselves: but they are under no obligation to relate these drawings to normal wage rates.

The arrangement in Mondragon is that the members deliberately limit their cash drawings to the equivalent of local wage rates, in order to re-invest any further earnings in the business. In Eastern Europe, laws require standard (government controlled) wage rates to be paid and any extra cash drawings are effectively prevented. In Hungary, however, the taxation rules have recently been changed to allow the members of small workers co-operatives (less than 100 workers) to distribute as much cash to themselves as they choose. As a result, the policy adopted by the members of those enterprises is to decide

*The Hungarians have a different solution. The General Assembly elects a number of small committees, the members of which cannot be members of the Directing Committee. These committees meet frequently and any member of the enterprise can apply to them. They deal with such matters as Supervision, Appeals, Law, Part Time Workers etc. The number of such committees tends to increase with the size of an enterprise.

their monthly cash drawings afresh at the end of each accounting period. A forecast is made of the net business earnings in the next period and of the amount likely to be required for re-investment at the end of it. Taking these factors into account, the members then decide on the rate of their cash drawings for that period.

This is an intelligent way of dealing with the problem. Members of worker-owned businesses should NOT proceed on the basis of first 'paying' themselves 'wages' and then regarding any business earnings left over as a 'surplus' available for re-investment.

Cash distributions can be divided between the members equally: but this is unusual. The normal practice is for the money to be divided on a 'job rating' basis in the same way as wage rates vary in conventional businesses .

Entrance Fees

The Mondragon organisers claim that a financial commitment to the business makes all the difference in the behaviour of worker-owners. Hence the Mondragon requirement of an entrance fee from all new members of an enterprise.* The East European organisations all make the same stipulation, although they differ in the amount of the fee and the period over which payment can be made. The requirements vary from one to three months' salary, paid in over a period of from one to three years. The Mondragon requirement is for a fixed sum from all members paid within two years. The sum is roughly equivalent to two months' earnings of the average member. The Mondragon organisers state firmly that this requirement can be met by even the poorest Basques.

Some people object to entrance fees on the grounds that it is wrong for workers to have to buy their jobs. That is perfectly correct. People should get their jobs on their merits as workers, without regard to any capital they may subscribe. This is how entrance fees are arranged in the Mondragon and Eastern Europe movements, where the fees can be paid out of a member's earnings over a period after joining. Life may be easier for a new member with some capital: but his ability to join, and his position at work, is unrelated to his capital assets.

The justification for entrance fees (apart from their practical desirability) is the need for new worker-owners to compensate members who leave for the assets which they must necessarily abandon, and which the new members automatically acquire. The point is further examined in Appendix I — Capital Holdings.

---

*It may not be practical to require this when the owners of a business are transferring it to its workers. However it is possible to name a specific period (five years?) within which all workers must either become members and pay their fee or take redundancy.

Capital Holdings

Conventional shareholders accept the decisions of their business directors to re-invest part of the business earnings, instead of paying them all out in dividends, because the shareholders know that this will increase the value of their shares when they come to sell on the open market. Some comparable arrangement is required to encourage worker-owners to re-invest part of their business earnings, instead of drawing them all out in cash. There are people who believe that capital should be held collectively, in which case worker-owners who re-invest in their enterprises must do so partly at least for the benefit of posterity. This is the principle generally accepted by ICOM in Britain, SCOP in France and the LEGA in Italy. However it is not the blue-print this book is following.

Most people find it both just and expedient for members who leave a worker-owned enterprise to be compensated for abandoning the assets which they have assisted in building up, particularly in paying entrance fees and in reinvesting part of their business earnings. The Polish and Mondragon organisations thus, quite separately, hit on the idea of 'capital credits' for members. Each member has a loan account in his business, which is credited with a proportion of his entry fee payments and of his share of any reinvestments of income. In Poland this pproportion is exactly half. Members get annual interest on their accumulated credits, which are paid out to them when they leave. They thus benefit only as lenders and only in proportion to their work in the business. There are detailed arrangements to allow members to withdraw their credits in exceptional circumstances and to discourage them from quitting the business in order to cash their credits.

There are possible objections to such capital credits schemes in other countries, and there are advantages in shareholding arrangements. Alternative schemes are therefore considered in Appendix I, one of which is adopted for the Model Rules in Appendix J.

Legal Rules

It has been made clear that, provided they conform to the definition of worker-ownership, individual enterprises and groups should be free to adopt such rules as they choose. However they will be required to register under the law, which means in practice company or corporation law or (in most countries) special co-operative law. In respect of company or corporation law the requirements of worker-owners are quite different from those of conventional shareholders. If a conventional shareholder has any legal problem, he goes to a lawyer: and what his lawyer requires is law of such precision that he can claim his client's rights without possibility of doubt. Company law is thus so complicated that only lawyers understand it. Worker-owners by contrast are present in their business and, in cases of doubt, can appeal to their fellow members for 'common justice'. What they require, therefore, is rules which are brief enough for all to read and simple enough for all to understand.

Rules of this nature are indeed available under co-operative law. Unfortunately co-operative law is normally based on so-called 'co-operative principles' which include requirements quite inappropriate to worker-ownership (see 'Co-operative Principles' in Chapter 9).* The suggested solution is to use whatever legal rules can largely be deleted after registration, and for the members then to draw up their own set of simple rules as a legal agreement between themselves. A 'model' agreement of this nature is given in Appendix J.

Summary

The members of an enterprise should have objectives on which all agree. The rules of their business should conform to the definition of worker-ownership. Within that constraint, their rules should give them practical democratic control of their affairs and should motivate them to act responsibly. The suggested way of doing this is —

CONTROL arrangements which comprise —

- a **General Assembly**, which is the sovereign body.
- a **Directing Committee**, elected by the Assembly.
- a **Management Board**, appointed by the Committee.
and in larger enterprises —
- a **Works Council**, elected on a 'shop' basis.
- a **Supervisory Committee**, elected by the Assembly.

CASH arrangements which comprise —

- **decisions** by the General Assembly at the end of each accounting period on the rate of cash drawings.
- **distribution** to the members (weekly or monthly) on the basis of their job ratings.

CAPITAL arrangements which comprise —

- an **entrance fee** commitment by members, payable out of their earnings.

* It is usually possible to word the rules required by co-operative law in such a way as to avoid their impeding the practical operation of a worker-owned business. However that makes it difficult for the members to understand which rules are intended to govern the conduct of their democratic enterprise and which are mere verbiage. This defeats the objective of having simple easily comprehended rules.

- **personal capital** holdings which take account of members entrance fee payments and of their re-investments of business earnings — and (possibly also) of the way in which they have conducted their business.

Further details are given in Appendix I (Capital Holdings) and Appendix J — Model Rules.

"A Group"

13 — Grouping

"We all depend upon each other: nobody can do anything single-handed but make a fool of himself" — E. Philpotts

Synopsis

General grouping idea is explained.

Federal Groups are necessary for finance and security.

Group Staffs have many tasks.

Education, Welfare, Social group arrangements.

Service Units are a necessary part of groups.

Job Security is obtained by means of grouping.

New Enterprises are launched by group staffs.

Business Combines involve fewer enterprises working more closely together.

General

It has been explained in Chapter 5 how worker-owned businesses can work together as closely as may be convenient: and it has been explained in Chapter 11 how the finance of worker-owned businesses depends on their operating in fairly large federated groups. The success of the Ularco combine has been noted under 'Mondragon' in Chapter 10: whilst the need to limit the size of individual enterprises has been explained in Chapter 12 under 'Democratic Control'. The resultant picture is one in which two phenomena appear —

a) One is the operation of worker-owned businesses in federal groups of sufficient size to have headquarters staffs able to carry out all the tasks required to secure borrowed capital. Their tasks may even include responsibility for such matters as social security and education. Such groups will not usually be of much less than (say) 10,000 people.

b) The other is the operation of worker-owned businesses in smaller combines, in which the member enterprises pool appropriate parts of their operations. This may be limited to such matters as accounting and transport, or it may involve integration of production and sales. The enterprises concerned always remain separate undertakings, the members of which give up an agreed amount of their sovereignty to their combine. Such combines can be of any size which the member enterprises may find convenient.

107

In order to differentiate between these two types of grouping, they are here described respectively as 'Groups' and 'Combines'. However there is no specific demarcation line between the two. The Federal Groups are the ones first described below.

Federal Groups

Wherever worker-ownership has been successful, the enterprises have got together in federated groups: and (as has been explained) these discovered how to initiate worker-owned businesses with capital borrowed from normal sources of finance. It is primarily the problem of finance which leads the member enterprises of a group to accept a degree of uniformity in their organisation and practice. The central staff of the group find that it is only safe to lend to enterprises which agree to operate in certain ways — for example with entry fees. Provided the staff express views generally agreed by the members of the group, these are made a condition for any enterprise which joins (or is launched by) the group. It follows that group staffs tend to be the people most concerned in the evolution of worker-ownership organisation and practice.

The central staff of a group is usually appointed by elected directors. Each enterprise in the group elects one or more members (according to the size of the enterprise) to form an 'electoral college', which then elects the group directorate. A group headquarters is funded by its member enterprises, either by a levy on their turnover or by charges for services rendered or through charging slightly more for loans than would otherwise be necessary — or by some combination of these methods. In Mondragon the members were lucky in having a prosperous savings bank to create the management division which has since become the group central staff. In Poland the co-operatives pay 1% of their turnover, partly to meet the costs of their group (and central union)staffs and to build up capital funds.

Groups normally form on a regional basis. However the staff of such a group has to be a 'jack of all trades': whereas, if groups are formed on a trade basis, they can have much smaller staffs which will be expert in their particular trade. Mondragon has remained a Basque regional group of 100 or so enterprises. In Poland in 1975, where there were some 1500 enterprises in regional groups, it was decided to rearrange most of these in trade groups. There were misgivings that some enterprises might thus find themselves far from their group headquarters, with communication difficulties. In the event however the new trade groupings were found to be a complete success. Unfortunately the Polish government soon afterwards decided to re-organise its local authorities in smaller units, with which the workers' co-operative organisation was required to liaise. This involved a reversion to regional grouping, although one or two of the trade groups were able to continue.

As already explained, the headquarters of a worker-ownership group

108

normally requires the member enterprises to agree to a number of rules which, in the opinion of that particular group, are necessary to success. It is likely that some enterprises disagree with some of the rules of their group: but the advantages of group membership are so great that the author knows of only one case in which a worker-owned business has seceded from a group.*

Group Staffs

The most important function of a group staff is that of creating conditions which allow it to lend money to the member enterprises with security. As explained in Chapter 10, this involves the normal hire purchase technique of only making loans to enterprises which are both commercially viable, and organised in such a way that their members will feel committed to servicing the loan. The group staff then has to provide the member enterprises with continuing advice and aid.

The following are the sort of activities which a group staff has to undertake —

- Finance has to be found and appropriately made available.
- Forms of enterprise organisation have to be evolved which motivate members to make a success of them.
- Long term planning is required in order to warn enterprises of expected future trading conditions, the possible need to plan diversification, and so forth.
- Financial monitoring of member enterprises is required, so that they may be warned of possible future losses or cash-flow problems.
- Managerial monitoring is required, so that enterprise directing committees may be warned of inferior managers.
- Major rescue operations will have to be mounted on occasion.
- New enterprises have to be launched.

In addition to the above, group staffs have to arrange for technical research, a central computer service, and (possibly) housing for members. The staff will normally set up separate units to operate these services to the group.

Education, Welfare, Social

In Chapter 3 under 'Capital Control' attention has been drawn to the possibility of a man doing the same work at the same level of skill all his life. It was also shown how the capital ownership system makes it very difficult for even the best intentioned managers to fulfil their workers by improving their skills. This situation changes completely under worker-ownership, where there is large expenditure on education. Thus the Mondragon group sets aside

*One enterprise seceded from the Mondragon Group because the members considered the group limit on differentials to be too low.

10% of any reinvested earnings in order to finance Basque-speaking schools, besides which it provides large support for the Mondragon technical college. In Poland in 1976 there were 90 technical schools with 1400 full- time and 1600 part- time instructors. In the smaller Hungarian organisation it is estimated that, in any one year, 40,000 ordinary members will receive some instruction in their enterprises and 3-4,000 managers will be receiving headquarters instruction.

Where more than one worker-ownership group exists, and where in consequence there will be a national headquarters, education is likely to be organised centrally. Otherwise it is a responsibility of group staffs. Education comprises instruction in technical skills, managerial skills and democratic procedures.

Welfare arrangements have been particularly interesting in Mondragon, because Spanish law originally excluded self-employed people from social security benefits and members of the Mondragon enterprises were (correctly) diagnosed as such. The Mondragon group thus had to set up its own organisation for providing unemployment benefit, sickness benefit and a health service. The resultant arrangements appear to have been better than anything provided by any government service in any nation. This example points to the way in which social security can be decentralised from governments to worker-ownership groups (where these come into existence) with benefit to all concerned.

The arrangement in the Mondragon group was that the members voted each year for the benefits which they wanted, taking into account their estimated cost. The group social security unit (set up by the group staff) then provided those benefits, informing the group members of their cost at the end of each year. The group members adjusted their social security subscriptions accordingly. This is an over simplified description of the arrangements: but these were summarised by a director of the social security unit, who said "and if these people were in the national scheme, not only would they have no say in deciding on costs, but they would never even know what these were". The advantage of local decentralised social services are that —

● people can choose how much they wish to pay for different types of benefit;
● benefits can be channeled to those who really need them;
● local financial responsibility prevents benefits being improperly drawn.

Social arrangements (if desired) can be run by units set up by the group staff, as for example a social club for Mondragon members in Bilbao. In Eastern Europe all the workers co-operative movements have large holiday organisations, mostly on a national basis but some run by groups. These parallel the holiday organisations of the different nationalised industries, which started after the second world war when the suppression of conventional private enterprise resulted in a general absence of holiday facilities.

Service Units

There are bound to be units in a federal group which cannot be fully worker-owned, because their only task is to provide services to the group. Such units comprise (for example) group staffs, research teams and computer operators. These may be able to make charges for their services: but, even so, the amounts they charge will depend on group decisions. There is thus a problem of motivating their members. This is dealt with by supplying the conditions discussed in Chapter 8. In other words, those concerned have to be made to feel that they are important persons doing important work.

The Mondragon planners have evolved two further arrangements. Firstly, they divide control of a service unit 50:50 between its members and the group as a whole. This arrangement is admittedly weighted in favour of the group, because the members of a service unit cannot operate without group agreement: but it does give them a measure of control over their own work. In the case of the Mondragon group headquarters staff, control is divided three ways. New directors of this staff are elected, one third by the staff members, one third by the existing directors and one third by the group as a whole.

The second Mondragon arrangement is that the cash drawings of the members of a service unit, and the annual additions to their personal capital holdings, are determined by the average of all the group members. This obviously encourages the members of a service unit to give good value to the group.

Job Security*

In order to provide capital loans with security, a group staff must obviously avoid the liquidation of any its enterprises. This fits in very nicely with the first objective of worker-owners (and therefore of their group staffs) which is to ensure security of employment. The policies evolved by the Mondragon staff to achieve these ends have, when applied over a period of years, had remarkable results. The group has weathered first a Spanish and then a world recession, without unemployment exceeding 1% and without any of its members ever receiving less cash than 80% of local wage rates. The factors which have contributed to this result are as follows:-

Firstly, it is worker-ownership policy to bring work to the workers instead of vice versa. A business enterprise may become uncompetitive because it is badly managed or because its methods of production are outdated or because the market for its products has contracted. In conventional industry the remedy is for its workers to move to more successful (often newer) enterprises. In a worker-ownership group by contrast, the remedy is to bring better management to the business or to provide the business with newer methods of production or to vary (or even completely change) its production. Capital for these changes may have to be provided. In extreme cases, successful

*See also Appendix M — Full Employment.

111

enterprises in the group may be asked to help by taking over (temporarily or permanently) some members of an enterprise in difficulty.

Secondly, it is axiomatic that the members of an enterprise sink or swim together. There is no question of making some members redundant so that the remainder may continue to draw full pay. In order to tide the business over its difficulties, cash drawings are reduced for all (at least temporarily) and hours of work may be increased. As stated above, this has never resulted in the members of a Mondragon business having to draw less cash than 80% of local wage rates.

Thirdly (and as already noted), job security is given precedence over maximisation of earnings. The result is that all concerned, and particularly the group staff, look a long way ahead. It used to be a rule in Hongkong that no new venture should be undertaken which would not repay its capital costs within five years. The fact that capitalist investors could not foresee events beyond five years was no bar to their setting up a business, if it could be sufficiently successful within that period. In Mondragon by contrast, a business is set up as a permanent institution: and it is the object of all concerned to maintain it as such for ever. One result is the consideration given to diversification, not only well ahead of any need, but as reserve planning against the possibility of such need arising. Looking forward in this way is an especial function of the group staff.

Fourthly, the joing together of most of the Mondragon group enterprises in appropriate combines (as described below) much increased their commercial strength — and correspondingly decreased the worries of the group central staff.

New Enterprises

A special task of group staffs is that of starting new enterprises. It is an observable phenomenon that, wherever worker-owned enterprises succeed, their members feel a desire to assist other people to do the same. So much is this so that, once a group of such enterprises is formed, it may be relied upon to devote time and money to this task. The problems for the group staff are those which have already been considered above: but, in a new venture, they arise in their most acute form. A good deal has been written on this subject. It suffices to say here that the Management staff of the Mondragon group likes to have as much as two years in which to prepare for the launching of a new enterprise.

Business Combines

As already explained, industrial democracy has been found difficult to operate in enterprises which exceed (say) two or three hundred people. However there is a natural tendency for successful worker-owned enterprises to attract more members. The problem of enterprises which were 'too big' thus arose in all the East European organisations, as well as in Mondragon (where the problem was high-lighted by the strike in Ulgor).

The Romanian organisation adopts an interesting practice, which is to allow the members in different branches of a large co-operative to elect their own local managers. This is usually done where the branch is physically separated from the other parts of the enterprise. It might be expected that locally elected branch managers would clash with centrally elected directors: but the Romanians make the system work. There is also the Hungarian practice of 'joint ventures': whilst the Yugoslavs have separate 'units of work' within a co-operative. However the arrangement evolved in Mondragon appears to be the best for adoption elsewhere.

In 1968 six of the enterprises in or near the town of Mondragon joined in a local combine, which they called Ularco. They elected a combine directorate, which appointed appropriate staff to take responsibility for the financial, legal, personnel and transport arrangements of the six combine members. The Ularco experiment was so successful that, in 1978, it was decided to recommend all the Mondragon enterprises to get together in Ularco type combines. After some natural objections by enterprises which disliked the idea of abandoning any of their own control of their own affairs, this took place.

Most of the resultant combines operate on a local basis, but some are on a trade basis. In this matter the same considerations apply to combines as to groups, except that distance is more important in the former. The Mondragon planners produced a set of rules for a combine, which were based on the practice evolved in Ularco: but the extent to which the different enterprises in a combine share their activities must obviously depend on circumstances. The point, as explained in Chapter 6, is that worker-owned enterprises can do this to any degree desired without losing their separate identity. They thus gain the strengths of a conventional business combine whilst retaining the motivating effect of being separate small enterprises.

Directors of conventional business combines often claim that the enterprises they acquire enjoy the same advantages. "We leave the local managers to run their businesses as they think best. All we do is to change the managers if they fail". However such directors ignore the possibility of their own failure and of themselves being swallowed by an even bigger take-over bidder. They also overlook the de-motivating effect on the members of their component enterprises of knowing that ultimate control of their business is in distant hands.

Summary

Worker-owned businesses naturally get together in groups which are large enough to employ substantial central staffs, whose task is to supply their member enterprises with advice and aid. This aid includes the setting up of separate units to provide specialised services to the group, which may even include the provision of social security. A competent group staff, as well as finding all the capital required by the member enterprises, can provide effective job security for all. This includes the members of new enterprises launched by the group.

In addition, enterprises within the group can (and normally should) join with each other in business combines, in which they work more closely together. Both groups and combines can be organised on either a local or a trade basis. In both groups and combines, the members of each business retain ultimate sovereignty over their own affairs. They delegate more control to a combine central directorate than to that of a group: but the extent to which they do so is a matter of agreement between the enterprises concerned in each case.

"Motivation"

14 — Motivation

"The best teachers do not profess to form the mind, but to direct it in such a manner, and put such tools in its power, that it builds upon itself" — Walt Whitman

Synopsis

Need for Motivation is explained.

Financial Motivation is important.

Financial Commitment is required from the start.

The Idea of Freedom is motivating.

Terminology can affect motivation.

Need for Motivation

It has been explained how managers of conventional businesses are required to make production for money their objective, how market competition then ensures their doing their best to achieve that objective and how, as a result, capitalist business owners need do no more than buy and sell their shares. The managers of worker-owned businesses, by contrast, have the much more complicated objective of fulfilling the lives of their workers: and there is no stock exchange to provide automatic indication of their success or failure in this task. It follows that worker-owners cannot, like conventional shareholders, just sit back and let management worry. They have to take active steps to keep their management up to the mark. Unfortunately worker-owners are human beings, and human beings are liable to be both lazy and short-sighted and thus to neglect their own best interests. It is therefore important for worker-owners to arrange their businesses in such a way as continually to stimulate themselves to worry about their management.

In this connection, although money is not their only interest, worker-owners are unlikely to be fulfilled in their work if their enterprises earn them appreciably less money than is paid out to comparable workers in capital owned enterprises. They thus have to make sure that they have managers able to compete commercially with conventional business managers, who are people chosen solely for their money making ability.

All this may seem obvious: but experience has shown that, once workers find themselves with leaders of their own choosing, they are inclined to leave everything to those leaders. They feel that, instead of having to watch capitalist managers who may do them down, they can trust their own managers to look after them. This attitude was one of the reasons for the gradual run down of the old producer co-operatives. Their managers failed to keep up with the energetic and progressive managers in capitalist employ, and their members were not sufficiently concerned to notice this until it was too late. The members of one producer co-operative even found that their manager had been selling some of their production on the side for his own private gain.

Financial Motivation

It has been explained in Chapter 3 how one of the great changes which worker-ownership will bring about is the discovery that people work in order to fulfil themselves. However, since most people have been brought up to believe that money is the object of work, money will for some time remain the yardstick of success at work. This applies particularly at the start of a new business, when the attainment of commercial viability is as important to worker-owners as to capitalist owners. Even after that stage, one of the factors which will attract people to adopt worker-ownership will be the sight of worker-owners making a lot of money. Hence the need for financial motivation in three ways.

Firstly, it is important for worker-owners to appreciate that they no longer live in a world in which they have any right to be paid anything. A fair days work no longer entitles them to a fair days pay. They get everything which their business earns (after paying interest on any capital loans) but, if their business earns nothing, they are entitled to nothing. Hence the importance of reviewing the rate of their rate of cash drawings at the end of each accounting period. This may normally result in no change: but the procedure should be gone through, in order to remind members of the connection between the progress of their business and the availability of cash to be drawn out of it.

In that connection there are two other points. One is that worker-owners should reject the custom of annual accounting.* The accounts of most small businesses can perfectly well be arranged so as to produce quarterly figures, even though it may not be worth while proving their accuracy with auditing and physical stock-taking. The other is that worker-owners should draw their cash monthly, if only so as to differentiate themselves from conventional wage earners. The idea that workers cannot be asked to accept this is absurd, when (for example) everyone in Spain is paid that way.

Secondly, worker-owners must be motivated to make appropriate re-investments of their business earnings. Conventional shareholders are happy to let their managers decide how much to reinvest in their business, because they know that any money thus diverted from dividend payments may be expected to increase the capital value of their shares. Worker-owners need

*Annual accounts are what auditors like: but it should be explained to such people that business accounts are kept for the information of the business owners, rather than for the convenience of the auditors.

118

some comparable arrangement, if their enterprises are to keep up with the rate of re-investment achieved by conventional businesses.

The reader will note here the de-motivating effect of any infraction of that part of the definition of a worker-owned business which excludes externally supplied equity capital. Nothing discourages reinvestment by worker-owners more than the knowledge that, if they make sacrifices to increase their future business earnings, part of the increases will have to be paid away to others who take no part in their work.

Financial Commitment

The need for an entrance fee commitment has been explained in Chapter 11 and the complementary need for some form of personal capital holdings has been explained in Chapter 12.

An entry fee distinguishes between those who propose to join a worker-owned business on a long term basis and those who are just looking for a job. It further commits the former to their decisions. It is not unusual for human beings to decide to make an effort towards some goal and then, when things do not go quite so well or so quickly as they hoped, to get cold feet and to want to abandon the effort. An entrance fee, together with a probationary period in the business, guards against this.

A personal capital holding is an important motivating factor, particularly as workers grow older. In 1970 a senior member of the French SCOP organisation remarked that, although one or two new SCOP enterprises were started each year, one or two established enterprises folded up. He said that the members of a SCOP business often made substantial sacrifices in starting it up but, over a period of time, this enthusiasm often seemed to run out.

It appeared to the writer that this was due to the lack of any effective personal capital holdings scheme in SCOP, similar to that in Mondragon. Young worker-owners can look forward to the future advantages of being members of a prosperous business. However as they get older, they begin to think more about the time when they will no longer have to work, and may instead enjoy ease and comfort. They remain concerned with the success of their business largely to the extent that it affects that future ease and comfort. If all they will get is a pension on retirement, there is no need for them to worry much about their current work: but, if they have a capital holding in their business, to be drawn out when they leave, they naturally continue their efforts to improve their business.

The Idea of Freedom

People are capable of being motivated by ideals, but only if the ideals suit them. Care must therefore be taken in presenting the aims of worker-ownership. Objectives which suit one person may merely annoy others.

Happily everyone can agree on the idea of freedom. Promoters of worker-ownership can thus all join in endeavouring to free people from capital control, even though they may disagree as to the ways in which the attainment of that freedom should then be used.

Worker-owners can (and should) be motivated by being told that they are part of a crusade to free people in industry. However this must be an addition to, and not in place of, appropriate financial motivation. What people like best is doing something which benefits themselves, and which at the same time earns them public esteem. Hence the Mondragon recommendation that a new worker-owned business should preferably produce something prestigious.

It can be difficult to present worker-ownership to people as providing them with freedom to do what they like, whilst at the same time telling them that they must adopt those practices which experience has shown will lead to success. It is claimed in this book that Mondragon practice, backed by that of Eastern Europe, provides a blueprint for successful worker-ownership operation. However prospective worker-owners should be told, not "this is how you do it", but "this is how it seems that you are most likely to succeed". It should be made clear that, provided they conform to the definition of worker-ownership, they can decide what they like about their own business.*

It follows that freedom should be the watch word in worker-ownership, both as a motivating ideal and as a practical reality. It is a pity that the term 'industrial democracy' is tarnished by association with the battle between capital and labour, so that it is often taken to imply more power for the workers to defy their managers. True democracy is both free and responsible, which is a situation that people in receipt of wages can seldom attain.

Terminology

Although no great change may appear to occur to people who become worker-owners, they have in fact entered into a whole new world of freedom. Experience shows that it often takes some time for them to realise this. The manager of a small firm which was taken over by its workers reckoned that it was about three years before most of the members really grasped the fact that they were in control. A comparable situation on a larger scale was the final establishment of political democracy in Britain by the passing of the Great Reform Bill. This gave power to 'the working classes': but it was only half a century later that they realised their power in the formation of the Labour

*The management staff in Mondragon tell a story of how they formed a low opinion of the leader of a group of prospective worker-owners. Consequently, before the business was started, they persuaded the members of the group to accept someone else as their manager. In the event, however, that manager failed and the original group leader took his place with great success. "Now", the staff say, "we give our advice, but we always tell the people that it is up to them to decide."

120

Party. It is important therefore, if worker-owners are to act intelligently and responsibly, for them to remind themselves of their new status by means of new terminology.

It is important also to try and avoid using words which no longer mean what everyone expects them to mean. It is explained in Appendix K how the word 'profits' changes its meaning in worker-owned businesses and how the word 'wages' is quite inapplicable. Hence a need to avoid using the former word without some added explanation and a need to substitute some phrase like 'cash drawings' for the latter word. The word 'surplus' is often substituted for 'profits'. However this tends to give rise to the misleading idea that it is the 'surplus' which is available for reinvestment. In fact, the amount which it is desired to reinvest should be considered at the beginning of an accounting period, and taken into consideration when fixing the rate of cash drawings for that period: so that the trading surplus at the end of the period is (as far as possible) a planned one.

Promoters of worker-ownership are inclined to be chary of abandoning the word 'wages', because they find that people are put off the idea of worker-ownership when they learn that they will no longer be paid wages. However it is doubtful if the spread of worker-ownership is assisted by inducing people to take it up without their really understanding its implications.

The Hungarians have an interesting custom. They give up use of the words directors and managers, on the ground that such people are pictured as 'capitalist lackeys' who oppress the workers. They use the word 'leaders' instead, which does accurately portray the changed status of management in worker-ownership conditions.

Summary

When the conventional system of running a business is abandoned, so also is the automatic motivation of management which the conventional system applies. Therefore worker-owners must themselves take action to get efficient and progressive management, if only to ensure that their businesses earn them as much as conventional ones. However worker-owners, being human, require arrangements which will keep reminding them of this. Hence the need for —

- procedures about cash drawings.
- entrance fees.
- personal capital holdings.
- appropriate terminology.

Worker-owners can also be motivated by the idea of freedom and, later, by the new possibilities which freedom will allow them to discover.

"Quantum Leap"

15 — Method of Change-Over

*"Nor shall my sword sleep in my hand till we have built
Jerusalem in England's green and pleasant land"*
— William Blake

Synopsis

Responsibility for Action lies with academics and industrialists.

Empirical Change-Over of a business is impractical.

Quantum Leap is necessary at the start.

Difficulties are explained.

The Hump at the beginning has to be surmounted.

Promotional Bodies are required to get over the hump.

Risk Capital has to be replaced by risk labour.

Workers' Bank is useful but not necessary.

State Subsidies are not required.

Large Scale blueprint is available.

Flip-Over from one system to the other will occur.

Responsibility for Action

In the complex conditions of modern societies it is difficult for a
fundamental change to be brought about by individual trial and error — as
was (for example) the change-over from the Roman to the Arabic system of
numerals. Basic change now requires conscious effort on the part of people
who see the need for it. In democracies, these people are not likely to be
politicians because democratic governments tend to follow, rather than to
lead, public opinion. In consequence the desirability of a change-over from
capital ownership to worker-ownership has first to be examined by academics
and (if recommended) then demonstrated by industrialists. Only after that
can ordinary working people be expected to take it up. It is therefore foolish
to reject the idea of worker-ownership because it is not demanded by 'the
workers'. Until its operation has been successfully demonstrated, how can
ordinary people tell whether such a system is what they want or not?

It is true that trade unions evolved without any theoretical planning: but
the immediate remedy for the dissatisfaction of workers was obvious to those
involved. Even so, we now see how much better it would have been if the
'leaders of industry' in the past had appreciated the need for collective

123

bargaining, and thus avoided the legacy of bitterness and ill-will which their opposition then has bequeathed to us today. Indeed, if the academics and industrialists of those days had understood the changes brought about by the factory age, they would also have understood the logic of the producer co-operative movement. Worker-ownership would then have been welcomed by all, and nobody would have bothered to read Karl Marx.

Empirical Change-Over

Business men normally prefer an empirical approach to change. "Let's see what will work in practice, before we go too far". Their natural idea is therefore to try giving the employees of a business some say in its control and some share in its profits. Then, if that works, the amount of their control and of their profit sharing can be increased until eventually the workers get full control of the business. The ultimate stage would thus be reached only when the workers had demonstrated their ability to cope with it. That is an attractive looking method for trying out and eventually changing over control of a business. There are however two insuperable objections to its adoption.

The first comes from the well-established fact that a human enterprise does not succeed under the control of two parties with differing objectives (see Chapter 2). This means that sooner or later there will be deadlock between capital and labour sharing control of a business. Then, either the business will fail or one of the two parties will succeed in getting control of it. This does not mean to say that naturally co-operative leaders of 'the two sides' cannot succeed in working together, or that capitalists and workers cannot cooperate in establishing the commercial viability of a new business: but, sooner or later, divided control is a recipe for failure. Managers, finding themselves required to serve two masters, will either behave as described in the Bible or will merely be inefficient.

The second objection is that workers will never act responsibly whilst they have less than full control of a business. Indeed they require all the motivational arrangements set out in Chapter 14. Failing these, they may cooperate with capitalists who create a prosperous enterprise able to pay high wages: but, as soon as difficulties arise, they will start listening to trade union activists who tell them how they are being done down by the capitalists.

These are the reasons why there is no blueprint in existence of the successful operation of enterprises in which control is divided between capital and labour.

Quantum Leap

In any one business therefore, the change-over has to be made completely or not at all. There has to be a quantum leap from one system to the other. This is not to say that a business owner cannot make the change by degrees, either by selling his business to his workers over a period, or by giving it to them but retaining ultimate control until they get used to their new role. However this assumes a benevolent business owner. In any conditions in which it is necessary for worker-owners to act without such assistance, they must have full control from the start.

As a result the spread of worker-ownership, wherever this has taken place successfully, has been almost always been by the creation of new enterprises. The possible alternative is the formation of worker-owned businesses to take over failed conventional ones. Such circumstances may make it is easier to get workers to consider the idea of worker-ownership: but it is probably harder to carry a failed business to eventual success, than to make a success of an entirely new one.

This position will change when a number of really successful worker-owned enterprises are in operation in any given country or region. Then the 'wage slaves' in other businesses may realise what they are missing and demand the right to buy out existing capitalist owners. However that is looking some way ahead in nearly all countries.

Difficulties

If, as would appear to be the case, worker-ownership has to be introduced mainly by the creation of (necessarily small) new enterprises, two difficulties arise.

The first is that it is precisely in small enterprises that there is least need for worker-ownership. Dissatisfaction, which will lead people to try out new ideas, exists in the 'dark satanic mills' of large scale industry rather than in small businesses. Indeed a major advantage of worker-ownership is its necessary operation in enterprises of limited size. Unfortunately it is impractical to introduce worker-ownership into the large undertakings where it is most needed, before it has successfully been demonstrated in small enterprises. This difficulty has to be suffered.

The second is that new enterprises are always very difficult to initiate. The standard capitalist technique is to accept the fact that many such ventures will fail, but to offset these against the large profits which are expected to be made from the few that succeed. That technique is of course quite unacceptable to worker-owners: and, as explained in Chapter 13, it is unnecessary when qualified group staffs exist to initiate new enterprises.

However that does not solve the problem of what is to be done where no groups of worker-owned enterprises have yet come into existence.

The Hump

In most Western democracies today worker-ownership is in a chicken-and-egg situation. On the one hand, it is necessary to have a group staff to give the necessary advice and aid to new worker-ownership enterprises. On the other hand it is necessary to create a lot of worker-owned enterprises before you can have a group of them. This results in a 'hump', which has to be surmounted before the opportunity of worker-ownership becomes reasonably available to the ordinary citizen.

The successful organisations in Spain and Eastern Europe only got over this hump in severe economic conditions, which provided a very strong incentive for people both to create and to maintain gainful employment. In the welfare states of today comparatively few people have the incentive to struggle through all the difficulties of establishing a new technique of business control in order to get themselves employment. Help is therefore needed.

Promotional Bodies

What is required is groups of business executives, with the skills necessary to the launching and subsequent nurturing of business enterprises, and with an understanding of the techniques of worker-ownership. This is indeed a tall order: and it is surprising that anyone has even attempted it. However, apart from the established organisations in France and Italy, there do exist such attempts — for example the Industrial Co-operative Association of Somerville, Mass, USA and several such organisations in Britain. This is the way forward, because the first essential for ordinary workers who wish to form a worker-owned business is someone to give them advice and aid. The object of any such promotional body should be to create enough worker-owned enterprises to form a group, which will then tke over the members of the promotional body as the group headquarter staff.

Unfortunately the existing promotional organisations are mostly too small (the Mondragon management division comprises some 100 executives), and their members often lack adequate business or even worker-ownership understanding. The danger then is that the enterprises which they create either fail commercially or fail to demonstrate real industrial democracy. Enterprises which fail in either of these respects do more harm than good.

Risk Capital

It usually appears to those attempting to start worker-owned businesses that capital is the great difficulty. However the real problem is that of producing enterprises worthy of being lent money. The requirement is for an appropriate mix of people, with a sound business plan, who are willing to undertake the sacrfifices which may be required to make their venture succeed and repay its capital loans. It is surprising how start-up capital can be found, from one source or another, if and when that requirement is met.

Of course a promotional staff is assisted by the availability of a 'revolving loan fund' capable of sustaining some loss. People cannot be expected to

126

succeed in promoting worker-ownership without making some mistakes, and hence some losses, at the start. However it is important for the controllers of any revolving loan fund to realise that their purpose is to establish conditions in which loan capiital will be secure. Whenever they make a loss, it will be because they have failed to ensure one or other of the conditions explained in Chapter 10, which require —

- that the business to which money is lent must be so organised as to commit its members to whatever sacrifices may be required to achieve success.
- that the venture is commercially sound.
- that the necessary advice and aid will be available.

These conditions may at first be very difficult to achieve: but the point is repeated that worker-owned enterprises which fail do more harm than good. They confirm the general opinion that "co-operatives" are not a practical way of running industry.

Workers' Bank

Seeing the success of the Mondragon Workers' Bank, people are inclined to think that a bank is what is wanted in order to promote worker-ownership. As has been made clear, it is not the savings bank in Mondragon but the management division which makes it possible for the enterprises to borrow all the capital they can usefully employ. Nevertheless a bank especially designed to lend money to worker-owned businesses can serve a useful purpose. This would be not so much to produce capital, as to provide valuable publicity.

The point has been made that many people in the Western democracies feel that there is something wrong with the conventional industrial system. Such people would welcome a chance of putting their savings where they would 'do some good' instead of into the 'capitalist system'. Consequently, given the same sort of terms as are available from ordinary savings banks, these people would prefer to deposit their money in a bank which would use it for the social purpose of promoting worker-owned businesses.*

The result would be a great increase of public interest in the progress of worker-owned businesses. There is no reason to suppose that such a 'workers bank' would be able to lend on better terms than any other bank — although the Mondragon bank in fact achieves this — but it could operate as a most effective propaganda machine. In that connection it may be noted that Basques who deposit their money in the local branches of the Mondragon

*Such a bank could only operate in conjunction with (one or more) appropriate management staffs, with the task of deciding when money could be lent to a worker-owned business with security. These would be the staffs of existing groups or the promotional staffs considered above. As in Mondragon, deposits which exceeded the possibilities of safe lending to worker-owned enterprises would have to be handled in the normal banking manner.

savings bank like to feel that it will be used to assist local worker-owned enterprises, rather than others further away.

State Subsidies

Protagonists of worker-ownership are liable to complain that prospective worker-owners are faced with a hostile industrial environment. However the apparent hostility arises from the facts, firstly that worker-owners cannot (if they are genuine) accept equity capital, and secondly that they cannot borrow capital until they can give it security. This makes finance at first hard to obtain. However, once worker-owners establish groups of enterprises able to give security to borrowed capital, they will be able to get all the capital they need and their environment will regain its normal normal state of neutrality.

This brings us back to the hump — how are prospective worker-owners to create the groups which will enable them to give security to loan capital? Here is a case for temporary state assistance. Unfortunately legislators tend to take the line that if, on the one hand, worker-ownership is not commercially efficient it ought not to be helped and that if, on the other hand, it is able to compete then it needs no help. At the same time conventional business owners object to (what they see as) rival enterprises being subsidised by the state.

The answer (it seems) is that, whilst the state should provide no permanent subsidy or special advantages to worker-ownership, there is a case for temporary state aid in getting over the hump. This will not penalise conventional businesses, because it will do no more than make worker-ownership as readily available to people as is conventional capital- ownership. When this has been done, the legislators can lean back and see which system people choose.

Large Scale

It has been stated that dissatisfaction with the existing system, and the need for worker-ownership, is greatest in large-scale industry. Hence the importance of the fact that worker-owned enterprises can work together in groups and combines (Chapter 13). These are the means which enable worker-ownership to be applied to enterprises of any size. The operation of combines of worker-owned businesses is strictly comparable to the way in which conventional business combines already operate. The difference in worker-ownership is that the directors at each level, instead of being appointed from above, are elected from below.

Let us imagine a vehicle-manufacturing enterprise which includes (say) five assembly plants, together with an engine and a body-making plant. Let us assume that each of these seven plants conveniently occupies a different factory. Then each of these would be operated by a separate worker-owned business, all seven of which would freely join together in a vehicle-production combine or federation. The extent to which the seven businesses would delegate part of their control of their own affairs to an elected central directorate would be a matter for joint agreement.

Such a combine would operate just as any conventional vehicle-producing business does now, with the one vital difference that the directors of each plant, and of the central board, would be seeking fulfilment for worker-owners instead of profits for capitalist owners. If the reader doubts the practicality of arrangements of this kind, then all he has to do is to go to Mondragon in order to see them successfully working.

It might be thought that a worker in one of the departments of such a combine would find himself much the same kind of 'cog in the machine' as he was before. However there are two great differences. One is that the worker-owner has control over what most matters to him, which is his own immediate environment. He and his friends can arrange it as they like. The other is that distant decisions which affect his environment and his earnings are taken by people 'on his side'. Being subject to the democratic process, their object is bound to be the benefit of the workers in the combine who elect them.

It might be thought that directors of the central board, subject to democratic control in this way, would find it difficult to make wise long-term business decisions. However, as has been explained, the evidence shows that this is not so. Worker-owners, even in comparatively large numbers, use their democratic powers with great responsibility.

Finally, it needs to be appreciated that organisations in Eastern Europe show how very large undertakings can be successfully operated under worker-ownership. Thus the Polish workers co-operative organisation of half a million members operates in three tiers, with the usual arrangement of elected directors in control of the executive at each tier level. This works as follows:-
At the lowest level, that of the individual enterprise, the members elect the directors of their business. The directors of all the enterprises in the group then elect the directors of their group headquarters: and the directors of all the groups in Polan in turn elect the directors of the 'national union'. It is obvious how such an arrangement could be applied to (say) a large nationalised industry in the West.

It can be argued that this sort of thing only works in an iron curtain country, where the workers have got do what they are told. However the Polish organisation was well tested by Solidarity. Although most of the Polish worker-owners strongly sympathised with Solidarity, they saw it as a movement irrelevant to their own organisation. This would not have been their attitude if the ordinary co-operative members had not been reasonably satisfied with their leaders. If the operation of industrial democracy in the large Polish worker-ownership organisation had been ineffective or phoney, the members would have taken an active part in Solidarity. They did not do so.

Flip-Over

We have all seen a see-saw, with a large grown-up on one end and children getting on the other end and gradually increasing its weight. At first the extra children appear to make no difference. Then, as more children get on, the see-saw suddenly flips over. This is the way worker-ownership is likely to progress. For quite a long time it will be a minority movement. However a point is likely to arrive at which ordinary people realise it to be a practical alternative to traditional employment for wages. At that point there will be a large change.

It may be argued that, given a fair wage, reasonable working conditions and trade union protection, the average worker is not going to put himself out by demanding fundamental change. However what is likely to happen is that conventional employment will become unfashionable. The question "Are you still working for a capitalist boss?" will make people vaguely ashamed of continuing in conventional industry. Then there will be a demand by workers to buy out the enterprises in which they work, which they will be able to do on a hire-purchase basis, and the demand for which will be irresistible. Industry, in any country in which this stage is reached, will then quite quickly flip over from one system to the other.

Summary

Worker-ownership requires to be initiated by academics and industrialists, before ordinary people can be expected to understand its advantages.

Since worker-ownership has so far been spread by the creation of new enterprises, and since this is best done by existing groups of enterprises, there is a hump to be surmounted in most Western democracies. This can be got over by the creation of promotional bodies, the members of each of which will be taken over as the headquarters staff of the group of enterprises it creates.

Worker-ownership should not be subsidised: but the state has a duty to make it reasonably available to ordinary people.

There is a pattern available for the application of worker-ownership to large scale industry. Provided its objective is maintained, worker-ownership will gradually progress until it becomes the fashion, when the remainder of industry will rapidly change over.

"Unfashionable to Work for a Boss"

16 — Economic Results

"Some see things as they are, and ask why? I see things that never were, and ask why not?" — Robert Kennedy

Synopsis

The Change will depend on people's demand for democracy.

Business Progress will continue as before.

Monopoly will be an increased danger, but avoidable.

Employment will be available for everyone.

Young Workers will want time to decide their future.

Industrial Training will be greatly expanded.

International business arrangements will continue.

Groups of businesses will be the norm.

Taxation of worker-owned enterprises will be different.

Exceptional Circumstances will be overcome by co-operation.

The Change

It has been stated in Chapter 15 that, when worker-ownership is seen to be a practical alternative to capital ownership, it will become unfashionable to work for a boss. There will then be a large change-over of business enterprises. It is then that worker-ownership will begin to impinge on a national economy. This is the stage at which large groups of worker-owned businesses will form, that people will begin to question their objectives in work, that unemployment will cease to be acceptable, that all will welcome the market, that the ownership of capital will begin to be really widely spread, and that rich worker-owners will be seen to be harmless.

The speed with which this stage is reached in different societies will depend on the commitment of their citizens to the idea of democracy. Although most people now subscribe to the idea of political democracy, many nations still lack it. Either their citizens fail to understand the principles necessary for its operation, or they lack the will to demand adherence to them. It is possible that some people will evolve the principles and practice of industrial democracy first, and then go on to demand political democracy: but the process is more likely to be the other way round.

133

Business Progress

It is explained in Appendix G — The Uncompetitive Market what happens when some worker-owned businesses are more successful than others, and how there will still be rewards which motivate producers to serve consumers. Industrial processes will thus continue to progress as it does now. However this progress will take place in the expansion, not of the more successful enterprises, but of the more successful forms of production.

If the picture of widespread business cooperation appears unduly optimistic it must be remembered, firstly that worker-owned businesses will have practically no incentive to poach each others sales, and secondly that they will operate in groups with headquarters staffs having the task of continuously finding improved forms of production and sales for their members. It may be that the more successful enterprises will not always welcome new entrants into their line of business (see 'New Entrants' in Appendix G): but the evidence of Mondragon and of the large East European groups is that problems of competition do not significantly arise.

It might be thought that, in the cosy conditions of worker-ownership, when no-one normally loses his job and when tough capitalist managers are replaced by elected leaders, work is bound to be less efficiently performed. This is not so. Firstly, worker-owners much dislike finding that other enterprises perform more successfully than their own, in which circumstances it is their management that gets blamed. Secondly, we see from Trade Union practice how effectively discipline can be enforced by workers' leaders if ocasion arises. Managers of worker-owned businesses (when correctly organised) are thus under as much pressure to perform successfully, and have as much disciplinary power, as their counter-parts in conventional enterprises. They will behave differently in one respect, which is that they will see success, not as a means of expanding their businesses for the benefit of shareholders, but as a means of increasing the earnings of themselves and their fellow workers. These inreased earnings will come, at first from higher prices (or lower costs) for what the business produces, and later from the receipt of royalty or franchise income. Managers will seek to become, not the appointed directors of business empires, but the elected leaders of worker-ownership combines and groups.

Monopoly

The public will benefit from the better or cheaper goods and services which managers endeavour to provide. However, in a system in which business enterprises mostly co-operate, there will be obvious opportunities for the introduction of monopolistic practices detrimental to the public. Thus groups of worker-owned enterprises, in which information and expertise is generally pooled, will also tend to exchange pricing details. This will provide a ready basis for price rings: and worker-owners, just like capitalist owners, will find life much easier if all agree to maintain high prices. It follows that more attention than now will have to be paid to anti-monopoly legislation. Further, such legislation will have to be extended to cover the changed circumstances of worker-ownership. Thus (for example) the state may have to limit the number of enterprises in any one trade which form· a single group. Other new problems will doubtless arise, calling for other new anti-monopoly rules.

Employment

Worker-ownership groups will become the main centres of employment. Polish experience (third para of 'Federal Groups' in Chapter 13) has shown that worker-ownership groups operate more effectively on a trade than a geographical basis. In such circumstances, vacancies in any particular trade will be best known to the groups operating in that trade. Similarly people wishing to start up a new enterprise will seek advice and help from the headquarters of a group in the trade concerned. The headquarters of worker-ownership groups will thus become the main employment agencies. It remains to be seen what will be done by governments in return for having most of their employment problems handled in this way. What is clear is that groups of worker-owners, besides helping each other, are always strongly motivated to assist people to join them.

It will be rare for a business enterprise to cease trading or even to reduce the number of its members, although its management and its production, and even occasionally its location, may change completely. As a result, people will normally work in the same business all their lives, and most new employment will comprise young people joining existing enterprises as replacements for those retiring.

This phenomenon — which seems so odd to us now — will only come about when most businesses are worker-owned. It is the interim period, when worker-owned businesses are still in the minority, which will be difficult. Later, it is quite possible that the operation of capital owned businesses will be restricted by the state.* When the majority of voters are worker-owners it may be argued that capital owned enterprises are anti-social because, by their natural seeking for growth, they are a threat to other businesses. Alternately, conventional businesses may be adequately restricted by the lack of labour willing to work for a boss'.

Young Workers

In assuming that most people will become worker-owners, exception has to be made of the majority of young people, who are likely to want time in which to decide exactly how and with whom they wish to commit their future

*The reader may envisage some very complicated 'company law' resulting: but it must be remembered that most of the present complications of company law will have ceased to be required by most of industry.

working lives. It is suggested in Mondragon that young workers do not become really committed to their enterprises before the age of 26-28. There is thus a case for allowing otherwise worker-owned businesses to accept non-member workers (paid ordinary wages) if under a certain age. Alternately there could be a spcial form of 'aspirant membership' for workers under a certain age.

Industrial Training

It is clear, both from Mondragon and from Eastern Europe that, once workers become worker-owners, they fully appreciate the advantages of training to increase their industrial skills. In all the existing organisations large sums of money are set aside for this purpose: and substantial training arrangements exist, both within each enterprise and at group and (where applicable) at national level. It is thus certain that, once worker-ownership spreads sufficiently widely in any society, the same thing will happen. Technical and managerial training for worker-owners always includes instruction in the operation of industrial democracy.

International

International businesses, although often given a bad name, perform a valuable function in spreading business expertise. In worker-ownership conditions, successful enterprises will still wish to benefit from exporting their expertise, whilst people in other countries will still wish to benefit by 'foreign' know-how. Happily, worker-owners will be able to benefit from the receipt of new processes from other nations (which may still be operating the capital ownership system) as effectively as conventional enterprises do now. It may be impossible for foreign businesses to set up subsidiaries in a state with a worker-ownership economy: but this problem already arises with nations which ban 'private enterprise'. It is solved by the payment of royalty or other fixed fees in return for the desired assistance. Thus, in conditions of worker-ownership, the Ford motor company of Britain (for example) may still bear the same name, and may still work closely with the parent Ford organisation in America, which may still gain substantial benefit from the arrangement: but that benefit will come from royalty or similar payments, and will not comprise any form of profits. In addition the policies of the British enterprise will of course be decided only by the operators of that enterprise.

Groups

Since the second world war there has been an increasing tendency for the formation of business combines, either in particular trades or in particular management styles. However, although the advantages of size are obvious, advantages are also claimed for 'small is beautiful': and management buyouts often show how parts of large enterprises can be more efficiently operated as separate undertakings. Happily, worker-owners can enjoy the advantages of both (as noted under 'Groups' in Chapter 10), so that their enterprises will normally all operate in groups and combines.

There will thus be further evolution of the ways in which such large undertakings are operated, and different management styles will continue to be widely discussed. However the objective of management will be, not merely how to increase the combine or group earnings, but how best to fulfil the lives of the people at work in it. The criterion of managerial success will be, not the number of investors wishing to buy shares, but the number of workers wishing to become members of the combine or group. There is likely to be keen competition between groups in the same trade for membership of the enterprises in that trade. The headquarters staff of any group from which enterprises secede, in order to join another group, will be in jeopardy of losing their managerial appointments.

Taxation

Once worker-owned businesses are seen to be a factor in any national economy, their taxation will have to be the subject of quite new arrangements.

The different incidence of wages and profits has been explained in Appendix K. Two points follow —

a) It will no longer be possible to levy taxes in relation to wages, as is done (for example) with PAYE in Britain. Such taxes might be linked to the cash drawings of worker-owners: but, since these can be varied by the members at will, it is unlikely that taxation authorities would find the arrangement satisfactory. An alternative might be to relate taxes to members' job ratings.
b) Taxes on profits will have to be levied on what would now be called the gross profits of a business, that is the profits before any money has been drawn out by its workers. The rate of such 'profits taxes' will of course have to be different from that applied to conventional businesses.

Account will also have to be taken of any financial burdens from which worker-ownership organisations relieve the government, such as unemployment relief and the organisation of welfare (see third para of 'Education, Welfare, Social' in Chapter 13).

Exceptional Circumstances

Since trade groups are likely to be the way in which most worker-owned enterprise get together, situations must be liable to arise in which the trade concerned suffers a major depression. Of course one of the tasks of a group headquarters staff is to foresee such a sitatuation. This is what the management division of the Mondragon Bank did in the mid-1970s, when it foresaw the coming depression in Spain and advised all the member enterprises to increase their exports: but such foresight may not always be possible. World politics can unexpectedly dislocate a particular trade, in which circumstances it may be beyond the resources of the group or groups concerned to get other forms of production going in time to keep all their members in receipt of reasonable cash drawings.

However, in a situation of solidarity with other worker owners, it is more than likely that those in different fields would come to their aid. Indeed examples of this happening already exist. In Eastern Europe, enterprises in a particular trade have on occasion been caught out by a sudden change in government policy. When this has happened the other members of the workers' co-operative organisation concerned have readily accepted the use of funds, which they had all helped to build up, to assist those in difficulty. This has meant keeping them in co-operative enterprises so as to save them from having to accept jobs in government industry.

Summary

The speed of change, to the point at which the effects of worker-ownership appear in the economy, will depend on peoples demand for democracy. Business progress will continue as before, but with the need to increase safeguards against monopoly. Worker-ownership groups will become the main employment centres. Young workers will require time to make up their minds. There will continue to be managerial discussion of the best ways of operating combines and groups, but with the changed objective of the benefit of their working members. There will be a great expansion of industrial training. International industrial expertise will continue to be available. Taxation of worker-owned businesses will have to be arranged on an enirely new basis. Worker-owners will help each other to meet sudden dislocations of trade.

"Social Results"

Chapter 17 — Social Results

"There is no sentiment in business" — Trad.

Synopsis

Social Unity will come about.

Labour Mobility will cease to be necessary.

Crime will be reduced.

Marriage will cease to be early.

Advertising will be much reduced.

Welfare will mostly operate at a local level.

Gambling will change its nature.

Sentiment will find a place in business.

Social Unity

It has been stated in Chapter 2 that it is the adversary situation in industry which is the cause of division between the rich and the poor in society as a whole. The 'poor' will view society differently when they are worker-owners. Firstly, they will see that all the profits of industry accrue to those who produce them, and that society contains no class of people 'battening on the workers'. Secondly, a person with low earnings will have to face the fact that these have been democratically decided by his fellow workers and, conversely, that people with riches will only have been able to acquire them with the agreement of their fellow workers. In these circumstances the poor may still feel hardly treated: but it will no longer be possible for them to identity any particular section of society (e.g. the rich) as being responsible. As previously explained, people with low incomes will regard those much better off than themselves with the same resignation as the plain girl regards the beautiful one. It may also happily turn out, when business earnings are distributed by those who create them, that the poor themselves can no longer be identified.

Labour Mobility

When worker-ownership allows industrial progress to take place without the liquidation of businesses, it will be abnormal for people to move their place of work after they have settled down.* It might be thought that, even

*The Mondragon authorities suggest that this is generally when a person reaches the age of about 28.

when not forced to move by redundancy, people would still tend to move over from the less to the more successful enterprises. However it can be seen in Mondragon that this is not so. The reasons are, firstly the measures taken to commit members to their enterprises ('Financial Commitment' in Chapter 14), scondly the willingness of worker-owned enterprises to share their expertise ('Two Firms' in Appendix G), and thirdly the duty of group staffs to help increase the eaarnings of any less successful enterprises ('Job Security' in Chapter 13). Worker-owners will thus normally remain members of the same business in the same location. This is not to say that worker-owners will never change their business or that a worker-owned business will never move its location: but such will be the exception.

The social effect of this lack of movement will be considerable, because it will produce a partial return to the conditions of the settled village communities, in which most people lived before the industrial revolution introduced the need for mobility of labour. It has been explained how business enterprises will become mutual benefit societies of freely associating people (third para of 'Business Societies' in Chapter 3). These people will naturally tend to live in the area of their place of work.* One effect of this will be a large reduction in the incidence of crime.

Crime

The reader may wonder how it was that there were no police forces before the industrial revolution. Wrong-doers must have existed in the past. Who was responsible for catching them? The answer is that, when people live in settled communities, criminals are easily detected.

Crime starts largely as a matter of experiment by the young, who only continue wrong-doing when they find that it pays. However in a community in which people mostly work together and know each other, the errant young soon get caught and find themselves subject to public disapproval. We can observe the result in distant lands to which 'civilisation' has not yet penetrated, where it is a rarity for anyone to commit acts inimical to the local society.

Of course modern industrialised nations, with large cities and the means of rapid transit, can never regain the conditions of small village communities: but, even so, a burglar (for example) will find it much harder to operate amongst settled communities of worker-owners. If he burgles within his own community, his neighbours will soon come to suspect him: but, if he goes outside his own community, he will be noticed as a stranger. Modern police forces will still be required: but the life of the criminal will be much more difficult.

*Of course there will be those who deliberately choose to live elsewhere, so as to avoid associating with the same people all the time: but they will be unusual.

Marriage

In most societies in the past, a man had to establish the means of livelihood before starting a family, because otherwise his family starved. Indeed many societies evolved customs which either required this or at least limited the possibilities of early marriage. Thus a Masai tribesman had to kill a lion before he could marry. The widespread custom, which still continues, of paying bride-price has the effect of limiting bridegrooms to men of some substance. In the past a Highland clansman in Scotland had to get the permission of his Chief before marriage, and this permission was normally withheld until the young man had land on which to raise a family. Societies benefit from arrangements which encourage their members to establish an economic base before having children.

At present, when it is possible for workers to be paid as much in early youth as they will ever earn, there is nothing to deter early families — often before those concerned are yet fitted to raise children. They acquire the necessary ingredients of a home by means of hire-purchase, because it is one of the advantages of youth to be able to live without serious inconvenience on a very low net income. A large part of their earnings is thus pledged in order to acquire TVs, cookers, suites of furniture and even houses. Young worker-owners, by contrast, will have an incentive to pledge their earnings to pay the large entry fees required by prosperous enterprises, which will later provide them with the means of raising a family in comparative affluence.* When worker-ownership thus provides ordinary people with the means securing their future, those who raise an early family instead of using their earnings to invest in a business will be regarded as improvident.

Advertising

Modern advertising plays a significant part in the lives of everyone in the developed countries. Some of the vast amount of advertising showered upon us is valuable in informing us of what is available; some of it is more or less harmless, and may amuse us; and some of it is actively bad, in attempting to mislead us or in distracting our attention from more pleasing subjects (such as views of the country-side). A large part of it absorbs money which would be better spent in other ways. Setting aside such contentious questions as to whether advertising induces us to buy things we do not need, it is hardly to be

*This may appear to clash with the point made in the previous chapter that young people may not wish to commit themselves to any particular enterprise until reaching the age of about 28. However it must be borne in mind that a worker-owner who wishes to leave a business can normally expect to take a capital sum with him, which will probably requite his entry fee payments. Although there will normally be penalties imposed on members who leave an enterprise soon after joining, it would be possible to rescind these for members still under a certain age.

doubted that we could do with a lot less of it. That is what worker-ownership will bring about.

Much advertising is put out by firms selling largely similar products, with the deliberate intention of misleading us into believing that the product advertised is better than the others. In fact the firm which has a better product than its competitors has that much less need to advertise. Advertising by capital-owned businesses arises from their need to seek more sales, or atleast to protect those they have. This arises in turn from the advantages of growth, explained in Chapter 5. When this incentive to business growth is removed by worker-ownership, advertising will be confined to useful information. An immense amount of money will then be released — for example to finance television programmes.

Welfare

The origin of the 'welfare state' was the Beveridge plan in Britain to provide national insurance against redundancy, with the premiums paid by everyone at work. However the original plan has long since deteriorated (in all countries) into a system of state hand-outs of various kinds, financed by general taxation. This is unsatisfactory for several reasons. There is wide disagreement between the citizens on the extent and nature of the hand-outs. These are often a hit-and-miss affair, with some people continuing to suffer hardship whilst others receive money which they do not deserve or need. The whole process (as explained in Chapter 7) is enormously expensive. Two main changes will come about in worker-ownership conditions.

Firstly, the remuneration of the less able members of society will be decided at group or enterprise level, where 'differentials' will be fixed. There will be no call for redistribution of incomes when these have been democratically agreed at source. Some people claim that it is the rat race which produces the most goods and services, and that earnings differentials should be appropriately wide. Others who claim that people will be happiest working together on the basis of 'from each according to his ability, to each according to his need'. There will be no need for these views to produce acrimonious disagreement at national elections. Like-minded people will get together in different enterprises and groups in order to put their different ideas into practice. In due course the best answers will emerge.

Secondly, the problem of misfortune will largely revert to genuine insurance arrangements at the level of worker-ownership groups, as demonstrated in Mondragon. It is inconceivable that democratic governments will continue to saddle themselves with welfare problems which groups of worker-owners will be able to handle so much more satisfactorily (see 'Education, Welfare, Social' in Chapter 13). The only state schemes needed will be for the minority of people remaining in the employment of private or state capital.

There is also the point that the general need for state welfare will decline when people at work are able to create their own capital reserves.

Gambling

The desire to gamble is — surprisingly — a valuable human trait, which has resulted in the exploration of the earth. People have an instinct to go and see "what lies beyond the ranges" (in the words of Kipling's poem), in the hopes of finding Eldorado there. Although this instinct has led many of them to their deaths, it has also led to many forms of discovery. However (as has been explained in Chapter 7) a person in employment forfeits his right to direct his own labour or to create his own capital. He may still 'strike oil': but, if he does so, it will be at someone else's behest and to someone else's profit. His inherited instinct is thus frustrated. Hence the provision of various artificial forms of gambling, which serve no useful social purposes.

One of the discoveries, made by these providers of gambling facilities, has been that people prefer their gambling activity to include some exercise of skill and effort on their part. Their instinct is to do something which 'with luck' will make them a fortune, rather than just to take part in a lottery. Worker-ownership will provide the outlet required by this instinct. Although security is the first requirement of people at work, when this security has been obtained groups of worker-owners will often choose to try out new and risky ideas in the hopes of 'striking oil'. Men's inherited gambling instinct will thus be diverted back again (from betting shops) to activities with a productive potential.

Sentiment

A general manager of a large business once said to the author — "It is a mistake to regard big businessmen as a lot of clever crooks. They are mostly quite honest and reliable: but they are heartless. They take no account of your existence as a human being." That opinion confirms the old adage that 'there is no sentiment in business'. This is not because businessmen are naturally callous, but because business competition requires them to concentrate on efficient production. This was the lesson learned by the managers of the competing businesses which arose in the changed circumstances of work produced by the industrial revolution.

Worker-owned businesses, by contrast, can survive without efficiency being placed above all else. This is not to suggest that worker-owners will normally tolerate either inferior managers or incompetent fellow workers. Indeed it is the managers of worker-owned businesses who are most likely to get the blame if things go wrong, and it is discipline enforced by workers on themselves which is the most severe. However worker-ownership makes it possible for people to mix justice with 'the milk of human kindness', without risking more than some reduction in their business income.

Thus (for example) John Smith may be liable to absent himself without adequate reason, to the detriment of the production in his business. In a conventional business John Smith would eventually find himself dismissed. However John may be a particularly likeable fellow with a great gift for telling funny stories, who is known to have unusual difficulties at home. His fellow workers may thus prefer some loss of business income to the dismissal of a member whom they like, and for whom they are sorry. Whilst worker-ownership is still the exception in industry and there are still conventional businesses waiting to take away the sales of any business which is less than 100% efficient, it may not be so easy for worker-owners to give sentiment preference: but, when most enterprises are worker-owned, their owners will be able choose between more business earnings and more kindliness to fellow humans.

Summary

Society will cease to be divided when the rewards of work are democratically distributed by those who produce them. When business enterprises remain in being indefinitely people will tend to live together in groups, which will reduce the incidence of crime. Most people will establish their economic future before starting to raise families, to the benefit both of themselves and of society. There will be a large reduction in the amount of advertising. People will need less 'welfare', and what is still required will mostly be arranged at worker-ownership group level. The human instinct to gamble will find its proper outlet in worker-owned businesses. It will again become practical for people to mix sentiment with business.

APPENDICES

Appendix A — PUBLIC OWNERSHIP

". . . state subsidised officials, who will fight like tigers to retain their status and their power" — William Paul

William Paul

"As capitalism enters upon its final stage the desire to control national production, the fear of industrial unrest, and the wish to enforce discipline on the workers will compel the capitalist class to extend state control. The extension of state control will bring with it armies of bureaucrats, who will only be able to maintain their posts by tyrannising and limiting the freedom of the workers. The nominal wages of the workers may rise, but it will be at the expense of their relative position in society and of their freedom. Within such a system, instead of being controlled by a handful of capitalists, the workers will be faced by a gigantic army of state subsidised officials, who will fight like tigers to maintain their status and their power. Such indeed is the logical outcome of state or national ownership. It is a social despotism organised from above." So said William Paul of Derby, who was one of the founding members of the British Communist Party in 1917.

What William Paul failed to foresee was the skill with which the bureaucrats would operate. So far from openly tyrannising over anyone, they take care in nationalised industries both to relax discipline and to accept pay rises, using the bottomless purse of the state to meet the consequent increases in costs. The result is to enlist the workers on their side, so that it is from the trade unions that there is open opposition to de-nationalisation. What the workers fail to appreciate (but what the bureaucrats must know) is that nemesis is bound in the end to catch up. No democratic government can find the money to subsidise nationalised industries for ever. It is certain that, sooner or later, either the government will call a halt or the citizens will call for a new government. Then the state has only three options — to make workers redundant, to put in very tough industry heads or to sell the industries back to private capitalists.

In this process, the bureaucrats may not appear to fight like tigers, but they succeed in producing a situation in which it is extremely difficult for their masters (the legislators) to unscramble an industry which has once come under state control.

Public Capital

As explained in Chapter 1, it is an illusion that workers can escape from industrial slavery by changing the identity of their capitalist masters. This is not because the state fails to have the best intentions, but because the citizens (who comprise the state) are just as remote from the enterprises which they control as are private shareholders. As explained in Chapter 2, the citizens may not expect profits like private shareholders, but they seek the reverse of the same coin which is the avoidance of losses. Hence they impose the same objective on their managers, which is production. It is true that at first, when industrial disputes arise, the citizens may be more inclined to give way than are private shareholders. However it is only a matter of time before they harden their hearts against demands for ever more money. Then the situation explained above arises.

It may be argued that this is an unduly pessimistic picture and that the state does (quite often) succeed in having contented employees in successful enterprises. However exactly the same can be said of private capital enterprises. Capital control of work does sometimes produce happy results, just as some slaves led happy and fulfilled lives in the old days. The point is that, if you are going to be a wage slave, the state is no better master than the private capitalist.

It may also be argued that the legislators could instruct the managers of state controlled industries to do what the citizens always say they want, which is to place the wellbeing of the workers first and increased production second. Then, when the citizens complain at inefficiencies in state industries, their government could say (in effect) "yes, but this is what you voted us into power to do." Unfortunately there is a catch, which is that any such arrangement would result in incompetent management. When production for money is the objective, managerial failure is obvious: but, if a manager can excuse any productive failure on the grounds of being nice to the workers, then there is no simple means of judging his ability.

It might be thought that this same problem would arise in worker-ownership: but the difference is that worker-owners, so far from getting government wages, receive only what their business earns. They thus demand competent, as well pleasant, management. The state manager with (supposedly) the same objective has no need to bother about high business earnings if he can substitute a high sounding line of hot air. This is something at which bureaucrats can be very skilled — which brings us back to William Paul of Derby.

Appendix B — HOPE FOR THE MASSES

"An idea for which he can live." — C. H. Malik

The following are two extracts from a speech made in the 1950s by Charles Habib Malik, when he was Lebanon's delegate to the United Nations:

"Those who see only the political, social, economic and military threat of communism miss its true challenge. When anybody in the West (who is not himself a communist or an appeaser) says that we can get along with communism then, either he does not know the nature of the thing with which he says we can get along, or — and this is the most grievous thing — he does not know the supreme values of his own heritage which communism has rebelled against and desired to extirpate. For I assure you it is not only your soldiers in Korea who are embattled today: it is the highest achievements of mind spirit and being of the last four thousand years."

"The balance of power must be redressed. However, unless not only the military balance is redressed, but also the European spirit develops an absolute faith in its values and a determined will to fight for them, I see no possibility for real peace. So long as Moscow means, truly or falsely, hope for the masses, it is idle to speak of live-and-let-live. For a man, no matter how weak or poor or ignorant, will be exceedingly strong and rich and wise if only he has an idea for which he can die, and therefore for which he can live. Communism provides such an idea. The communists have a purpose in life beyond their immediate cares and worries. The non-communist world does not have such a sense of mission. A mighty living true faith must be discovered or created to balance the militant faith of communism. He does not know the infinite positive hidden riches of the non-communist world in Asia, Europe and America, who does not believe that such a faith can be released in it."

Since that speech was made, the military balance of power has been largely redressed and there is a better understanding of the paucity of communism. However no great 'hope for the masses' has yet been released in the West. Happily it is not necessary to find anything quite so grand as the 'mighty living true faith' proposed by Mr Malik. History shows that freedom is an idea for which people will die and, therefore, for which they will live. The trouble is that the Western world is still only half free. The requirement is to complete that freedom by providing it for people at work.

151

Appendix C — THE WASTE OF CAPITALISM

"For all who believe in human values this is the real indictment of the system" — Ibid

In Britain in 1924, the Trades Union Congress and the Labour Party produced a document entitled *The Waste of Capitalism,* from which the following is an extract:

"The individual worker has become in most cases a mere cog in the machine, a pawn to be moved hither and thither by someone in authority who is carrying out a policy which the subordinate does not only not help to determine, but the very nature and objects of which are hidden from him."

"The worker goes into the factory, takes his meals and leaves again at night at fixed and stated times, all to the sound of the siren, while the exact period of his attendance is accurately and mechanically registered."

"He performs his allotted task on the instructions of a foreman, does it by following a definite stereotyped set of operations, in the determination of which he has no hand and may indeed violate all his instincts of craftsmanship and good work. If he does anything which is not laid down in his employers schedule he may be bullied, fined or discharged. There he is, to his own seeming a feeble unit in the hands of a huge organisation which takes no account of him as a human being. He is merely one of the 'hands' helpless to affect his environment to the slightest degree."

"Is it any wonder that the worker does not feel inclined to wear himself out producing more and more profits for his employer? The wonder is rather that production continues at all: and, in fact, there is no guarantee that it will continue under such conditions. Unrest is growing, not decreasing, and there is likely to be more and more friction and less and less production as time goes on if a remedy is not found. For years this tendency has been reinforced from several directions. On the one hand there has been the ever-increasing specialisation and more minute sub-division of labour with the progress of invention and the development of the automatic machine, so that the organisation itself has become rigidly arranged and disciplined. For economic reasons we have seen the formation of huge combines, mammoth undertakings which necessitate a still more mechanical soulless regime with more authority for those at the top and more 'discipline' for those at the bottom. Yet, at the same time, there has been an ever-rising standard of education for the workers, which has helped to produce the demand for a higher standard of life and a wider conception of the value of human personality."

"The average employee today has little of no interest in his work or in producing maximum output, partly because the work itself is so often drudgery and partly because he sees the organisation (in whose power he is) producing goods, the quality and quantity of which someone else has settled, the mode and manufacture of which someone else has planned, under working conditions someone else has decided — all to make profits for someone else. He is not asked to use his own intelligence or judgement, his own craftsmanship or artistic feeling, his own methods or theories. He is not asked to make suggestions about the enterprise as a whole, and in any case he has no fraction of share in the power of deciding whether any suggestion should be carried into effect. Manufacturing policy, commercial policy, financial policy — all are forbidden territory to him. His only share in the enterprise is to be a slave of the owners and to do what he is told, on pain of walking the streets as one of the unemployed. For all who believe in human values, this is the real indictment of the system."

"The sane human being has the desire to create, to use his own intellect and powers to change the material things around him, to effect his environment in the way his own nature dictates. It is these desires and fundamental instincts that the present industrial system frustrates, and in doing so stultifies itself: for it is part of the irony of things that in putting profits above humanity, the employer is in danger of destroying, not only humanity, but the profits themselves."

These prophetic words were written soon after the first world war, when Britain still thought of herself as 'the workshop of the world'. Half a century later, the reader will note the accuracy of the forecaste that "if a remedy is not found" there is likely to be "more and more friction and less and less production as time goes on".

Appendix D — DISUNITY AT WORK

"That workers in all industries do see employers as their opponents cannot be doubted" — Ibid.

The Class Room

When we are children we have to accept the authority of teachers at school. Inevitably therefore we divide ourselves into 'them', the teachers, and 'us', the school children. This does not mean that we necessarily dislike our teachers: but they are not 'us'. In dealing with them, therefore, we learn that we have to abide by a special code of 'school child' behaviour. This attitude changes if we go to university, where we first get the idea of 'the masters' being there to help us. However, if we go straight from school into a job in conventional industry, the feeling of 'them and us' may persist through life. This is what the following quotations show:

● "Our rules of behaviour had the tacitly understood code of manners and courtesies which have close paralells with the rules of the class room

— you cover up for your mates, and never on any account say anything which might get them into trouble, i.e. do not sneak.
— you never work competitively in ways which will show up your mates, i.e. do not be a swot.
— you take care never to appear superior to your mates, i.e. do not swank."

● "If for example the manager arrived and asked for Smith — who might not have appeared on the site for days and might even have held up your own work — you said "he's just nipped out for materials". If an individual was accused of shoddy work, you tried to confuse the issue so that everyone accepted collective responsibility."

● "There was one man who often slacked, which threw extra work on to the rest of the team. I was allowed to hear their complaints because, although I worked in the manager's office, I was only a girl: but, if the manager himself appeared, nothing was ever said. This was despite the fact they disliked the man in question and would have been glad to be rid of him."

Working Together

Trade union leaders and business managers can (and sometimes do) work amicably together: but it is very easy for one side or other to do something wrong which will arouse mistrust and suspicion:

● "Having watched Roy's careful and methodical approach to a job, and knowing that he had wasted no time at all, I felt aggrieved by the

154

manager's attack on him. However Roy told me that I had to get used to that kind of thing."

- "Most of his time Harry had been very happy, because 'the bloke who owned the firm had been a good guvernor, and we'd helped him out because he'd always treated us fairly'. But Harry's old guvernor had died, and the firm was taken over by a new manager, a pushy individual with no emotional attachment to the trade or to the workmen."

- "That workers in all industries do see employers as their opponents cannot be doubted. Certainly some employers run their factories in a more benevolent and far-sighted way than others: but workers have learned the lesson of their own history, which is that 'business is business'. They see it as natural that an employer wishes to make money out of their work: and, for this reason, their relationship with their employer is one of struggle for division of the spoils. Coal Board officials complain bitterly that any change they introduce is always greeted with mistrust. Scores of examples could be given of the prevailing idea amongst workers that any suggestion from management, since it is bound to be designed for greater profit, is likely to be some underhand attack. Coincidence of interests is unthinkable, and they cannot conceive of the boss being philanthropic."

- "That was when my career as a shop steward in Fords came to an end. Amongst my suggestions was one which would result in more efficient working of the production line, without any inconvenience to the workers. The chief shop steward was a friend of mine and he explained my error to me. "You see", he said, "management is the enemy: and the moment you proposed anything to assist production you forfeited all confidence by the other shop stewards". He advised me that I could never again hope to be made a shop steward."

- "About five years ago we tried to get the shop stewards interested, but they just didn't trust us."

- "Automatically, if management said they would give us another £10 a week, I couldn't help it but I would immediately start looking to see where the snag lay."

- "You could not help noticing if machinery was idle or if there was a slack period in the packing room or if a couple of salesmen were made redundant. In this atmosphere of uncertainty, trust disintegrated and the merest suspicion could throw management and men into battle array."

Honesty

Individuals, who would never think of stealing from each other, adopt a much lower standard of morality towards a capital-owned business which employs them. Use of the telephone for private calls is almost standard practice. The following quotations enlarge the point:

- "There was a certain tolerance of dishonesty denoted by the word 'fiddle'.

The managing director's new Jaguar was a 'fiddle'; the sales director's expense accounts were a 'fiddle', as were all management perks and privileges. A 'fiddle' was not necessarily something to condemn."

- "In the end nearly half of a stock worth several thousand pounds had disappeared. No one in management was allowed to discover this until it was too late, because loyalty to ones mates, even if you do not even know their names, is meant to supersede loyalty to employers."

- "When I started my own business I remembered how the bosses used to treat the men, and I decided I'd try and rule by kindness: but I soon found I was being swindled. So now I rule them with a rod of iron. I don't like doing it, but I can't make my business pay any other way."

Trade Unions

It is sometimes claimed that it is trade unions which cause all the trouble in industry and that, given a free choice, few workers would join them. However, in Britain in August 1980, although a MORI poll showed that

— 31% of trade union members disagreed with their union policy, and
— 59% thought the closed shop a threat to individual liberty, and
— 58% thought the unions had too much power, nevertheless the poll also showed that
— 90% thought trade unions essential to protect workers' interests.

The following quotations exemplify the feeling that, whatever the faults of trade unions, they are necessary for workers:

- "Harry himself had reservations about belonging to a trade union. "You wouldn't be able to pick up a broom and sweep after yourself", he pointed out, "because there'd be a special bloke for that". However this did not contradict the general opinion that you got nowhere with management unless you had the power to fight them. "That is the only thing management understands", opined Eddy, "and that's what the unions are really for". All agreed that workers require a union behind them."

- "but, when a strike was threatened by the union, I found myself called up to the board room — the first time a representative of the workers had ever been up there."

Stick & Carrot

Some people believe that workers are motivated primarily by the stick and the carrot and, therefore, that it is largely a waste of time trying to persuade them to cooperate. They believe that, if workers get good pay they will accept firm discipline, which is all that any manager can expect. However the following quotations do not bear this out:

- "He told me he liked the job because of the variety of challenges it

156

presented to him. It was certainly nothing to do with his wages, which were very nearly as low as mine. His energy and enthusiasm for everything he undertook infected us all. We were probably the most contented people in the building, and possibly the most creative. We were certainly the lowest paid."

- "When I first arrived, nobody questioned me about myself, made any visible effort to suit my talents to the job they were offering or tried to learn of my aspirations and ambitions. Nobody suggested any prospects no matter how dim, or tried to enthuse me with the history, the aims or the prospects of the firm. They were not bad employers: but it had not occurred to anyone that employees, who had invested their skill and labour in a firm, had as vital an interest as anyone else in its performance."

- "I think that most of these financial incentives are over-done. Of course finance affects people, because we would all like to have more money. But undoubtedly, beyond a certain level of money, what makes these people tick is a feeling that they are creating something and that, if they were not here, you would miss them."

- "It's more important to British people to be treated right than to be paid properly. They will work into the night if you ask them to help" said by a German executive working in Britain.

Appendix E — JAPAN

"The old order changeth, yielding place to new"
— Alfred, Lord Tennyson

It is the theme of this book that the capital ownership system is an anachronism in modern industry and the cause of all our troubles. However Japan appears to be an exception. Japanese industry flourishes and there is no deep division between Left and Right in Japanese society. Have the Japanese then evolved some special technique of operating the capital ownership system in modern industrial conditions? If so, why can't the rest of us do it too?

Paternal System

Prior to the industrial revolution most people in most countries worked on the land in an essentially paternal system. People were expected to take their place in an agricultural hierarchy of which the local landowner was the head. He had a duty to give them work and they had a duty to support him. Landowners (or workers) who failed in these duties suffered social ostracism. Perhaps it was not all quite as neat as that: but the idea of 'redundancy' was unknown. Then came the industrial revolution, with people being employed in small competing factories. At first the owners of a 'family business' tried to be responsible for their workers: but, whereas a landowner always needed workers to cultivate his land, a factory owner's need for workers varied with his success or failure in selling his production. The new factory owners thus soon found that any attempt to keep more workers than were required to meet their current sales merely spelt disaster for all. The old idea that an employer was naturally responsible for his workers was thus gradually replaced by the notion that 'there is no sentiment in business'.

However all that was a century or more ago. The picture in Western Europe and America has gradually changed, until today many people are employed in (comparatively) large corporations and combines with much more power to retain them in employment. Industry is also more stable — for example bank failures are now hardly known. Unfortunately the old idea of employers and employees having a duty towards one another has also died out. If employers do try to avoid declaring redundancies, it is probably for fear of provoking a strike. If workers do refrain from a strike, it is probably because they doubt its success.

In Japan, however, the change from an agricultural economy to large-scale modern industry took place in almost one jump. Big business undertakings thus appeared in Japan before people had lost the tradition of 'paternal' employment: so that many Japanese workers were able to continue the practice of serving one employer all their lives, to whom they gave their

158

support. Hence the happy position in large-scale Japanese enterprises of co-operation being the norm, rather than the exception — and it is widely agreed that this co-operation between masters and men is the secret of Japanese industrial success. If Japanese firms have more machinery per worker, it is not because their counterparts in Europe and America have not wished to do the same. It is because Japanese workers have accepted high rates of business reinvestment, in place of demanding the maximum possible wage settlements.

Of course this situation cannot apply to small Japanese enterprises, of which there are plenty. All the same, the idea of cooperation between the workers and owners of a business reaches them too: and there has been a carry over into industry of previously interlocking social structures, which has had some effect in reducing the vulnerability of small businesses in Japan.

Not for Export

It might be thought that large enterprises in Europe and America could copy the Japanese example: and some may even do so. Unfortunately the general adoption of this idea is hardly possible outside Japan, for three reasons.

In the first place, the successful functioning of paternal business enterprises requires people with a tradition of that pattern of behaviour. However, outside Japan, the industrial pattern has long since become one of a balance of power between employers and unions. Most workers would find it strange indeed to be told that they should cooperate with their bosses and accept 'reasonable' pay settlements. This was of course the way in which industry was intended to operate by those who advocated state control: but it entirely failed to work out.

In the second place, the idea of democratic control of people's affairs is now very deeply rooted in the West. So much is this so that 'paternalism' has become a dirty word, related in the public mind to dictatorship. It is quite true that people who accept wages accept dictatorship: but they mostly do so on the basis of having trade unions to oppose the dictators. Consequently, if there is to be change in industry, only a change to some democratic system would now be acceptable in the West.

In the third place, it remains to be seen whether the paternal system will necessarily continue in Japan itself. As affluence increases in Japan, so is it likely that people will be affected by the fundamentally divergent interests of capital and labour. It may be that the capitalist owners of large Japanese enterprises already receive no more financial reward than the rates of fixed interest which worker-owners would have to pay to service borrowed capital. However that does not provide the workers with the opportunity to create their own capital, nor does it allow them to decide their own objectives in work.

Appendix F — MAYNARD KEYNES

"It is an extraordinary example of how, starting with a mistake, a remorseless logician can end up in Bedlam" — J. M. Keynes (writing about another economist).

The Theory

The views of Maynard Keynes resulted from the great Wall Street stock market collapse of 1929, which set off a world trade depression. Keynes saw that, although millions of dollars of money disappeared almost overnight, there was no immediate reduction in goods and services. This reduction only followed when people stopped working, which they did because they could not get as much money for their produce as before. This was because the effect of the stock market crash had been a sudden decrease in the amount of money in circulation.

The British government of the day, finding itself faced with a 'trade depression', adopted the classic remedy of reducing its expenditure. However the effect of this was to reduce still further the supply of money and thus to deepen the depression. "The government", said Keynes, "is doing exactly the wrong thing. The requirement is to keep up the production of goods and services, for which purpose the government should be increasing the money supply instead of decreasing it". Keynes thus formed his theory of 'priming the pump' at the onset of a business recession, as a means of preventing the recession from spreading.

Keynes was absolutely right. As explained under Recessions in Chapter 4, there is no reason why people should stop exchanging goods and services just because there is a variation in the supply of the token we call money. The simple solution is to let incomes (and hence prices) rise or fall as necessary, as a result of which no one will be materially any better or worse off. However Keynes was living in the real world, in which it was (and still is) impractical to reduce the wages which comprise most people's incomes. His alternative solution of an artificial increase in the money supply was an equally effective remedy.

The Keynsian theory thus was that, when a decrease in the money supply began to start a depression, the government(s) concerned would borrow money with which to increase expenditure. In other words deflation would be countered by inflation. Then, in the favourable business conditions which would follow, the government(s) would recover their borrowing by a decrease in expenditure. Keynes had noted the tendency of business confidence to go in cycles, the ups and downs of which his policy would iron out.

160

The Practice

Unfortunately Keynes' theory was not put into practice until after the second world war, in conditions which were generally not those he had envisaged . Keynes' theory was based on two background assumptions. One was that the problem was to deal with a reduction in demand, resulting from a decrease in the amount of money in circulation. The other was that wages would remain stable. If it was impractical to lower wages in order to counter a depression, Keynes naturally assumed that no one would think of raising them in a depression.

What happened was that economists imbibed Keynes' theory of demand, without realising that it naturally assumed stable wages. At the same time legislators adopted Keynes' theory of priming the pump, without bothering about un-priming it when increased employment followed. Had Keynes lived, it is hardly to be doubted that he would have modified his teaching to take account of these factors.

In Keynes' absence by death, legislators resorted to pump priming when no recessions threatened, partly because every government was afraid of unemployment, and partly because they were urged to increase demand in this way by a (not very intelligent) new breed of economists. The effects were at first excellent. The populace paid little attention to the small degree of inflation which resulted and the workers were happy with full employment accompanied by small wage rises. However the process was like drug taking. The more you had, the more you needed.

As a result it did not take many years for the rate of inflation to increase to the point at which the workers realised its effect. At first inflation had given them the illusion of getting richer, without their realising that they were only getting more money tokens. In fact workers who merely maintained their wage rates actually got poorer. However, once inflation began to be discounted in advance in wage bargaining, the whole theory of a government increasing demand by increasing the money supply broke down. People were horrified to discover that they had both inflation and unemployment at one and the same time.

161

Appendix G — THE UNCOMPETITIVE MARKET

"Virtue is rewarded" — Trad.

Two Firms

In Chapter 5, an example is taken of firms A and B competing in the market for sales of the same goods. It is explained that, in conventional industry, a slight operating advantage on the part of Firm A will allow it to undercut Firm B's sales to such an extent that, if the advantage is maintained, Firm B will end up in liquidation. This is a severe penalty for a comparatively small difference in efficiency. It is further explained how this situation arises in conventional industry for two reasons, firstly because of the advantage of growth to capitalist business owners, and secondly because of the need to pay fixed wages. Let us now see what happens to Firms A and B when they are worker-owned, and when Firm A gets the same slight advantage:

a) The workers of Firm A will get themselves slightly increased earnings, either by selling their goods at a higher price, or by producing their goods at a lower cost, or by producing more goods at the same cost. Whichever may be the case with Firm A, the workers of Firm B will not suffer more than a slight decrease in their earnings. This may be unfortunate for them, but is neither unjust nor disastrous.

b) However the members of Firm B will naturally want to do whatever clever things are being done by Firm A, to whom they will offer an appropriate royalty or other payment in return for their know-how. This will be readily accepted by the members of Firm A, because they will gain no advantage from taking on more worker-owners in order to increase their own production. Firm A members will thus have some increase in their earnings and Firm B members some decrease: but it may happen the other way round next time.

c) The consumers will then be in the same position as if Firm A had got all the business, because both firms will have adopted the new process. In other words, the absence of damaging competition between worker-owned firms does not prevent new processes from spreading and benefitting consumers.

d) Of course it is possible that the members of Firm B will refuse a reasonable payment to Firm A, in which case Firm A may well invite a new collection of worker-owners (Firm C) to pay for and operate their new process. This situation would be bad for Firm B: but it will only rarely arise.*

*As is explained in Chapters 11 and 13, worker-owned businesses will normally operate in groups: so that Firms A and B will either be in the same group or their interests will be taken care of by separate groups. In either case there will be people who will knock their heads together and insist on their coming to a reasonable agreement.

Competition

People find it difficult to believe that industry will continue to serve consumers as well as it does now, if 'the spur of competition' is removed. However worker-ownership will merely bring back the conditions which existed before the industrial revolution. Individual workmen then vied with each other in pleasing their customers, because those who were most successful got the highest prices. As a result consumers were just as well served then as they are now. Thus (for example) cobblers all strove to produce the best shoes, because those who succeeded got paid the most. However the more skilled cobblers had no incentive to prevent their less skilled brethren from continuing to produce less good shoes at less good prices. Worker-owned businesses will behave in the same way for the same reasons. The only difference in modern industry is that individual businesses have replaced individual workmen as the units which serve consumers. The managers of conventional businesses now seek to please consumers because, if they fall behind in market competition, they lose their jobs. However the managers of worker-owned businesses will equally lose their jobs if, through failing to please consumers, they fail to provide their business owners with as much money as is provided by other more successful managers. The spur to management will be the same: but its application will no longer require business enterprises to damage each other.

New Sales

When one business enters a market in which it has not previously made sales, this is liable to reduce the price of the goods or services being supplied by existing traders in that market. In such circumstances even worker-owned businesses will be liable to damage each other. However, firstly this is a very necessary process for the protection of consumers, and secondly such damage need never be serious.

Producers normally only want to enter a market when they see that it is providing its suppliers with a higher reward then usual. However such a market normally exists because of some innovation. The innovators supplying that market will thus have been substantially rewarded before fresh producers come in. There is also the point that fresh producers do not normally enter a market if their additional production is likely to reduce the market reward below the average: and, if the rewards for any particular form of production do fall below the average, producers tend to leave that market — until its rewards rise again. Thus, although a market provides greater reward for innovators, it also operates so as to keep evening out all the rewards of work. Producers are not seriously damaged by this aspect of 'market competition': so that, although it will apply to worker-owned businesses in the same way as it does to conventional businesses, the point is not important.

The Balance

Consumers require, firstly that there should be higher rewards for producers who serve them better, but secondly that these higher rewards should gradually be reduced. Producers require, firstly that they should always be able to work, secondly that they should get higher rewards for innovation, but thirdly that they should be protected from having to work for rewards which are lower than the average in relation to their particular skills. As we see, a free market operating within a worker-ownership economy meets all these requirements, because:

● since they receive increased rewards for innovation, producers are stimulated to serve consumers better.
● this process does not put other producers out of work.
● innovative ideas get spread throughout industry.
● the market continuously tends to average the rewards of work.

The picture of worker-ownership industry is further considered under 'Business Progress' in Chapter 16.

Appendix H — THREE FAIRY TALES

"Once upon a time . . ." — Trad.

The First Tale

Once upon a time there was a man called John Mugg who lived in the land of Slavery, which was ruled over by ogres. Each ogre kept as many slaves as possible to grow food for him: but, if he had too many, he ate those that were redundant. The ogres thus depended for their food, partly on having a lot of slaves and partly on being able to eat them if necessity arose.

Now the ogres were all democrats, accepting parliamentary control of their affairs. The number of slaves an ogre might keep thus depended on his success in influencing the operations of the parliament. If the parliament required a reduction in the number of his slaves, it was unfortunate for the ogre (and even more so for his slaves): but the ogres accepted this because they were firm believers in a parliamentary system. It is not surprising, however, that the slaves thought otherwise. The parliament appeared to John Mugg and his friends as the main cause of their being eaten.

One day John Mugg escaped to Freeland, where he begged the citizens of that country to lend him some gunpowder so that he might destroy the parliament in Slavery. However the citizens of Freeland thought that John had the wrong idea. "Surely", they said, "it would be better if, instead of destroying the parliament, you got rid of the system of slavery which gives the ogres power over you?"

"Oh but", said John, "the ogres would fight to keep their slaves, on whom their livelihoods depend."

"Then", said the citizens, "why not avoid a fight? You could offer the ogres an agreed amount of food for the use of their land, which would give them greater security than being dependent on the workings of the parliament. You and your friends could then become democrats yourselves and use the parliament for your own benefit."

"WHAT", said John, "me become a democrat and have a parliamentary system? Why, democrats are wicked people and the parliament is what makes us redundant and gets us eaten."

"Don't be silly", said the citizens, "it is the system of slavery which does all the harm. When that is abolished, you will find that a parliament is the best method of political cooperation between people: and, when you no longer have to work for ogres, you will value a system which enables you to choose your own leaders."

The citizens tried hard to explain this to John: but he would not listen. He had been so much affected by his upbringing in the land of Slavery, that he could never believe any good of a parliament or stomach the idea of being a democrat.

In the end John got his gunpowder and went back and destroyed the parliament, although he damaged a lot of his fellow slaves in the process. However, when democracy had thus been abolished, the cleverest of the slaves got state control and acquired a taste for human flesh, so that life in Slavery was even worse than before. This did not matter to poor John, because the controlling slave disliked any talk of Freeland and made a point of getting John killed and eaten at an early stage.

The Second Tale

Once upon another time there was another man called John Mugg who lived in the land of Employment, which was ruled over by employers. Each employer kept as many workers as possible to make money for him: but, if he had too many, he sacked those that were redundant. The employers thus depended for their living, partly on having a lot of workers and partly on being able to sack them if necessity arose.

Now the employers were all capitalists, accepting market control of their affairs. The number of workers an employer might keep thus depended on his success in influencing the operations of the market. If these required a reduction in the number of his workers, it was unfortunate for the employer (and even more so for his workers): but the employers accepted this because they were firm believers in a market system. It is not surprising, however, that the workers thought otherwise. The market appeared to John Mugg and his friends as the main cause of their being sacked.

One day John Mugg escaped to Freethink, where he begged the citizens of that country to lend him some revolution so that he might destroy the market in the land of Employment. However the citizens of Freethink thought that John had the wrong idea. "Surely", they said, "it would be better if, instead of destroying the market, you got rid of the system of wages which gives the employers power over you?"

"Oh but", said John, "the employers would fight hard to retain their their workers, on whom their livelyhoods depend."

"Then", said the citizens, "why not avoid a fight? You could offer the employers agreed rates of interest for the use of their money, which would give them greater security than uncertain profits dependent on the workings of the market. You and your friends could then become capitalists yourselves and use the market for your own benefit."

"WHAT", said John, "me become a capitalist and have a market system. Why, capitalists are wicked people and the market is what makes us redundant and gets us sacked."

"Don't be silly", said the citizens, "it is the system of wages which does all the harm. When that is abolished, you will find that a market is the best

166

method of economic cooperation between people: and, when you no longer have to work for employers, you will value a system which enables you to create your own capital."

The citizens of Freethink tried to explain all this to John: but he would not listen. He had been so much affected by his upbringing in the land of Employment that he could never believe in a market or stomach the idea of being a capitalist.

In the end John got his revolution and went back and destroyed the market, although he damaged a lot of his fellow citizens in the process. However, when the market had thus been abolished, the cleverest of the workers got state control and developed a taste for dictatorship, so that life in Employment was even worse than before. This did not matter to poor John, because the controlling worker disliked any talk of Freethink and made a point of getting John declared 'an enemy of the people' and liquidated at an early date.

The Third Tale

This is the only proper fairy tale, because it is the one with a happy ending. It is about a man called John Smart, who also lived in the land of Employment and who also escaped to Freethink. However, although John Smart was a worker like John Mugg, he was less prejudiced by his upbringing: and so he listened with a more open mind to the citizens of Freethink.

"You see", said the citizens, "the merit of a market system is the way it marries production and consumption without coercing either producers or consumers. A market enables consumers to express their preferences, and it then rewards producers exactly to the extent that they meet them. If you abolish a market, firstly you abolish the only effective means of valuing goods and services, and secondly you apply coercion (under the name of 'control') to both producers and consumers."

"But", said John, "I am controlled by a boss in my factory. Isn't that coercion?"

"Yes indeed", said the citizens, "and that is just what is wrong. The trouble with your land of Employment is that, although you take part in the market as a consumer, you are excluded from it as a producer. What you want is freedom, not from the market, but from employment."

"Then", said John, "I shall have freedom to starve!"

"No no", said the citizens, "if you take part in a market you need never lack remunerative work, because a market always provides a reward for people who put anything into it. The amount of the reward depends, of course, on the skill with which you produce what other people want."

"But that's not true", said John, "because the employers take part in the market: and yet they often fail to sell their produce, which is when they make us poor workers redundant."

167

"That only happens", said the citizens, "because the employment system distorts the proper functioning of a market. A market is a means of exchanging goods and services, and the more of these which are put into a it, the more there are to take out of it. Since the people of developed countries now produce an immense range of goods and services which can be got to market, they can all get themselves remunerative work. This fails to take place in Employment for two reasons:

- Firstly, you and your friends are rewarded, not with the exchange value of the goods you produce, but with wages. The trouble is that, if these wages are high enough to give workers a fair share of the earnings of most businesses, they will be too high for some businesses to pay.
- Secondly, an employer normally gets more money the more workers he employs. This results in fierce competition for sales, which makes workers in the less successful businesses redundant. They are supposed to move over to the more successful businesses: but the process is far from pleasant for them."

"By contrast", said the citizens, "worker-owners seek, not growth, but increased income per worker. This enables worker-owned businesses to join together for mutual support, in which circumstances (believe it or not) redundancy for workers and liquidation of businesses enterprises need hardly ever arise."

"That sounds lovely", said John, "but, if we own our own businesses, some of us might decide that we preferred to earn less money and have a 30 hour week. What would then happen to the consumers?"

"Don't worry about that", said the citizens, "because when people take part in a market system both as consumers and producers, the amount which different collections of workers consume is determined by the amount which they produce. In your system of employment, by contrast, you get a fixed wage irrespective of what you produce — and only then if you're lucky enough to have a job!"

"That sounds fair enough", said John, "but I still don't like the idea of becoming a capitalist".

"Don't worry about that either", said the citizens, "because capitalists become harmless people when they no longer have power to control other people at work. May we add that there are detailed answers to all the other questions you will think up by tomorrow."

"My dear John", they concluded, "go back to your land of employment and get your fellow workers to run their own businesses. It is only in their own enterprises, operating in a market economy, that people can have real democratic control of their own working lives."

"OK", said John, "I'll have a go."

Appendix I — CAPITAL HOLDINGS

"Property is the first reality of freedom" — G. W. F. Hegel

Capital Credits

This appendix assumes that it is both just and expedient to make an arrangement for worker-owners to benefit personally from the business assets which they create. It is further assumed that the best way of doing this is for a member to receive a capital sum when he (or she) leaves the business, related to the increase in the capital value of the business which has taken place during that person's membership. Such an arrangement is clearly just: and it is expedient because it encourages members to put capital into their business, by paying entry fees and by refraining from drawing out in cash all the money their business earns.

For this purpose broadly similar schemes were evolved in the Polish and Mondragon organisations.* They were evolved quite separately and they differ in detail: but the following outline applies to both —

● When a member joins and pays his entry fee, he has a personal credit account opened in the business, in which he is credited with about half of his entry fee payment.
● Members only draw out in cash the equivalent of local wage rates.† All additional earnings are retained in the business.
● At the end of each accounting period, the total money thus retained in the business is divided (on paper) between the members according to their job ratings and each member's personal account is then credited with about half that amount.
● Should there be a deficit instead of a surplus at the end of any accounting period, members personal accounts are debited instead of being credited.
● Members are paid an annual rate of interest on the current total in their accounts. Whenever a member leaves (after an initial period of membership) his accumulated credit total is paid out to him in cash.

The Industrial Co-operative Association in America operates a variant of this idea, in which a member starts to get repayment of his credits after six years, so that the capital re-invested in the business constantly 'rolls over'.

*Out of the five East European countries in which worker-ownership organisations exist, it is only in Poland that the idea of personal capital holdings has been accepted.
†In both countries these are based on limiting cash drawings to the current rate of wages paid in comparable capital owned business. However in Mondragon this limitation is self-imposed, because the Mondragon members wish to accumulate capital with which to provide other Basques with jobs in worker-owned businesses: whereas in Poland (as in France) the government requires cooperatives to pay standard wages.

Although the Polish and Mondragon capital credits schemes are successful, and are likely to continue to be so, there are possible objections to their adoption elsewhere —

- Where a fixed sum has to be paid out to each member who leaves, a danger is bound to exist that the business will not have the necessary reserves available when the need arises. It would obviously be better to have a scheme in which this could not happen.
- Prospective worker-owners are liable to be discouraged by a scheme based on the idea that cash drawings will always be limited and consequently that, however successful the business may be, its owners will always have to wait until they retire before benefiting from their success.
- Members gain no benefit from hard work and wise decisions, however much these may have contributed to increases in the capital value of the business.

Share Scheme

The most effective way of giving worker-owners a share in the capital assets of their business is for each member to buy a 'share' in it at its current value on joining and to sell that share again at its current value on leaving. At the end of their membership individuals will then benefit (or otherwise) in accordance with the work which they and their fellow members did, with the re-investments of business earnings which they made, and with the decisions which they took. Such an arrangement need not contravene the rule of definition which requires worker-owners to receive benefit only in accordance with the work they supply, if it is arranged that shares are held by all members either equally or in accordance with their job ratings. Variations in the value of members shares will then always be related to the work which they have supplied.

A share scheme, in which new members are required to buy an appropriate shareholding on joining, also has the advantage of ensuring that the business is never required to pay out to members leaving more money than will be matched by the members who take their place.* Such a scheme also has the effect of committing new members to an entrance payment, which will come out of their earnings over a period. If share values are high, requiring large payments by new members, this will normally be matched by large earnings distributions.

Such an arrangement requires a valuation of the shares in the business by an 'arbiter' whenever members join or leave. These valuations will of course be based, not on any book figures, but on the value of the business to the people who join in its ownership. This is the kind of thing which is constantly done by financial advisers to investors on the stock exchange. It may appear

---

* If no members are taking their places, then the business is likely to be running down. In such circumstances it will not be judged (by the Arbiter) to have much value and little money will be needed to pay those leaving.

very complicated to an arbiter acting for the first time: but arbiters will soon gain experience of the factors requiring to be taken into account. An arbiter may often wish to put a good value on a business, so as to benefit members who leave: but he will have a duty to protect those who join, and values will necessarily have to be acceptable to prospective new members.

A detailed example of such a scheme appears in the Model Rules in Appendix J.

Possible Objections

There are three possible objections to the above share scheme, as follows:

Firstly, some people may object to the idea on the grounds that workers should not be asked to "buy their jobs". However it has been explained, under Entrance Fees in Chapter 12 'Operation', that this is not what happens when these payments are correctly arranged.

Secondly, it may be objected that this share scheme is liable to prevent a worker-owned business from ever building up its assets, because any increases in the business assets are constantly taken away again by the members who leave. However it is easy for the members to make a rule that those who leave the business will be paid only (say) 80% or 90% of the valuation of their shares, so as gradually to increase the permanent assets of the business.

Thirdly, it is claimed that the capital value of a worker-owned business may become so high that new members will be unable to buy a share in it, and the National Freight Corporation (NFC) in Britain is quoted as an example. However, if the monetary value of a worker-owned business increases, this will normally be because it makes more money available to its owners. If it fails to do this, then its value (to potential new owners) is unlikely to increase. The money which becomes available to new worker-owners during their early membership (when they are paying for their shares out of their earnings) will thus normally be commensurate with the current value of the business.

The confusion about the National Freight Corporation, and similar enterprises, arises from the facts:

a) that the NFC did not become a real 'worker-owned' business.

b) that a conventional business varies its value to a greater extent than does a worker-owned one.

In regard to a) above the NFC was de-nationalised and its shares largely sold to its workers: and, within a few years, the market value of those shares had increased thirty times. However not all the workers bought shares, which were in any case allocated according to the money paid. The workers thus acquired ownership in their capacity as suppliers of capital instead of in their capacity as suppliers of labour. The enterprise did not therefore become worker-owned in any meaningful manner.

The explanation of b) above stems from the point (made under 'Business Growth' in Ch 5 The Market) that capitalist business owners depend for their reward on the margin of business earnings remaining unspent after payment of all outgoings, including wages. Thus for example, if a conventional business just breaks even and has no margin of profit, it has no current value to its capitalist owners: but, if the same business is worker-owned, it will have appreciable value because its worker-owners can draw amounts of money out of the business equivalent to standard wages. The profits (and hence the sale value) of a conventional business thus start later, but thereafter increase much faster, than do the profits of a worker-owned business.

The reader will see from the two points above, firstly the need to have a definition of a worker-owned business (explained in Chapter 9), and secondly the need to understand the change in the incidence of 'profits' (explained in Appendix K).

Entrepreneurs

A difficulty with the general problem of starting new worker-owned businesses is that an entrepreneur may object to 'giving away' shares in an enterprise which is based mainly on his ideas and his leadership. Some of the most valuable people in industry are the individuals who have an idea, set up a business to put the idea into practice and then lead the enterprise to success. Such people should get a fair reward. An entrepreneur can arrange this in a worker-owned business, firstly by allocating to himself a comparatively large share of the earnings distributions, and secondly by giving himself an appropriate contract of service as chief executive of the business. This latter will not prevent the members of the business from electing whom they like to the Directing Committee: but it will prevent the members of that Committee from sacking their chief executive without paying him a very large sum. Of course the entrepreneur will have to get these arrangements agreed by the first members of the business: but, if those people see that the business is primarily the brain-child of the entrepreneur, and if they think that they will all benefit from joining him, they will agree.

An entrepreneur will thus gain all the advantages of having working partners in place of paid employees, whilst still getting effective security of office and a major share of the business success.

Appendix J — MODEL RULES

"What man needs is not law alone, nor liberty alone, but each in its own province" — Bertrand Russell

As explained under Legal Rules in Chapter 12, worker-owners require easily understood rules which they can interpret themselves, rather than precise rules which give security in a court of law. For this purpose their rules must be simple and to the point. Company and corporation law is normally far from simple, whilst the 'cooperative' law available in most countries requires the inclusion of certain phraseology which is pointless (and therefore muddling) for worker-owners. Hence the advice that worker-owners register their enterprises under any laws which allow them to cancel most of the provisions after registration, and that they make the operating rules of their enterprise in the form of an agreement between the members.

The following "Model Agreement", with its accompanying Notes, is designed to inform worker-owners of the various matters requiring consideration rather than to serve as a precise model. It covers the most complicated case, which is that in which the members decide to have individual shareholdings. If worker-owners prefer a system of 'capital credits', they can study the Mondragon or Polish models: and there is also the scheme evolved in the USA.

In the Model below the words 'employed by the company' are used because they have a convenient legal meaning. Factually, of course, the members of a worker-owned business are self-employed.

Articles of Agreement

between the

Members of _____ Worker-Owned Company

Principles *(note 1)*

1) The principles on which the Company shall be conducted are:

   a) that ownership and control of the Company shall be confined to those employed by the company.

   b) that not less than 90% of those employed by the Company shall be members of it.

   c) that the rights and benefits of the members shall be related only to the work which each supplies to the Company.

   d) that all externally supplied capital shall be borrowed by the Company.

Membership *(note 2)*

2) A person shall only be admitted to membership of the Company after:

   a) being employed by the Company for six months. *(note 3)*
   b) approval by the General Assembly.
   c) agreeing and signing these Articles.

3) A person shall cease to be a member of the Company whenever he or she resigns, is dismissed, dies, is absent from work for more than 3 months or ceases to be employed by the Company.

4) A member of the Company may be dismissed from membership by a two thirds majority vote at a general meeting. *(note 4)*

General Assembly *(note 5)*

5) Decisions at General Assemblies shall be by majority vote. Each member shall have one vote: and, in the event of a tie, the Chairman shall have a casting vote. A vote shall be taken secretly if required by 10% of those present.

6) A member may appoint any other member as his or her proxy at a meeting by giving written authorisation.

7) The first General Assembly shall elect a Chairman, who shall be responsible for the conduct of business at meetings and for ensuring that proper Minutes are kept and safeguarded. He shall hold office until a new Chairman is elected by a General Assembly.

8) The Chairman shall call meetings as he deems necessary or whenever requested by a quarter of the members.

9) A quorum shall comprise 90% of the members or their proxies *(note 6)*. If a quorum is not present, the meeting may be re-convened after 24 hours when those present shall form a quorum.

10) The Chairman shall give not less than 24 hours notice of a meeting by whatever means he deems satisfactory. *(note 7)*

Directing Committee

11) The General Assembly shall elect a Directing Committee of *(note 8)* persons to direct the business in accordance with General Meeting decisions.

12) The members of the Directing Committee shall serve for *(note 9)*, at the end of which period they shall be eligible for re-election.

13) The members of the Directing Committee shall receive no remuneration for their office, but they shall be eligible for overtime in accordance with Article 23.

Management Board

14) The Directing Committee shall appoint a Management Board of *(note 10)* persons with such powers and duties as the Directing Committee may decide.
15) The members of the Management Board shall be members of the Company and shall serve at the discretion of the Directing Committee *(note 11)*.

Works Council *(note 12)*

16) The General Assembly shall divide the members into separate constituencies, the members of each of which shall elect one member to a Works Council.
17) Members of the Works Council shall be given access to the Directing Committee and the Management Board, so as to enable them to provide constant communication between their constituents and the Committee and the Board.
18) Works Council members shall have no remuneration for their office, which they shall hold at the discretion of their constituents.

Supervisory Committee *(note 13)*

19) The General Assembly shall elect a Supervisory Committee of 3 persons to inspect the accounts and other records of the business, as they may see fit on behalf of the members. They shall hold office at the discretion of the General Assembly.

Earnings Grades *(note 14)*

20) Each member on admittance shall be allotted an earnings grade number by the Directing Committee.
21) A member's earnings grade number may be varied at any time by the Directing Committee.

Cash Distributions

22) The General Meeting shall decide, from time to time, how much money shall be drawn out of the business *(note 15)* for regular distribution to the members according to their earnings grade numbers.
23) Individuals who work longer than the other members may be made overtime payments at the discretion of the Directing Committee.
24) Sums of money distributed to the members under Articles 22 and 23 shall be entered in the accounts of the Company as wages and so treated for fiscal purposes *(note 16)*. Any persons working in the business who are

not members of it shall enter into a wages contract with the Company in the conventional way.

Capital Holdings *(note 17)*

25) The members of the Company shall share in its ownership according to their earnings grade numbers: and, in the event of its dissolution, the assets of the business shall be shared between them in those proportions.
26) Except in the case of the original members *(note 18)*, any person admitted to membership of the Company shall undertake in writing to pay for his share of the the current value of the business according to his earnings grade number. This undertaking shall include agreement to his payment being made by deductions from his cash drawings under Article 24 at the rate of 3% per month of the total payment agreed. Any member who fails to allow this to be done, and who fails to make the due payment by some other means, shall be deemed to have resigned his membership of the Company.
27) Whenever a member ceases to be a member and ceases to be employed by the Company, he or his heirs shall be entitled to be paid the current value of his part ownership of the business according to his earnings grade number, but subject to the terms of Articles 28,29,30. *(note 19)*
28) If a member ceases to be a member before his payments due under Article 26 have been completed, the amount due to him under Article 27 shall be multiplied by a fraction comprising the amount of the payments he has made to date divided by the amount he was due to have made under Article 26.
29) If a member ceases to be a member within 5 years of taking up membership of the Company, the amount otherwise due to him under Article 27 shall, at the discretion of the Directing Committee, be reduced by one half. *(note 20)*.
30) A member whose earnings grade is changed shall pay to, or shall be paid by, the Company the sum necessary to accord with his new grade number in accordance with Article 26. *(note 21)*

Capital Valuations

31) The General Meeting shall appoint an Arbiter to determine the current value of the Company. The Arbiter shall value the Company on the basis of its value to members, or prospective members, of it. *(note 22)*
32) At the end of each accounting period or whenever requested by the Chairman of the General Meeting, the Arbiter shall state the value of the Company. The value of each member's share shall be the amount of the latest valuation of the Company multiplied by the earnings grade number of the member and divided by the sum of the earnings grade numbers of all the members.

Amendments

33) The members in General Meeting shall be entitled to amend or add to or delete any of the Articles of this Agreement at any time by majority vote. *(note 23)*

Interpretation

34) In the event of any doubt or disagreement as to the interpretation of the terms of this Agreement, the matter shall be referred to the members in General Meeting, whose decision shall be final. *(note 24)*

NOTES

on

Model Agreement

Principles

1) *These principles are designed to ensure that the worker-owners of the Company have the same degree of ownership and control of the Company as would conventional capitalist owners. Where the law being used comprises Memorandum and Articles, it is suggested that these Principles are part of the Memorandum.*

Membership

2) *These rules are designed to implement principles a) and b).*
3) *You do not want people to become members of the Company until you (and they) are quite sure that they will fit in.*
4) *It only leads to trouble if you keep people working together who really dislike each other. It may seem hard that a person should thus be deprived of membership: but, of course, he will be paid the capital value of his share on leaving.*

General Assembly

5) *These rules are designed to be the minimum which will ensure democratic control of the Company by the members.*
6) *It is assumed that all members will attend General Meetings, either in person or by proxy, and the figure of 90% is stated only to allow for someone's arrangements to attend going wrong unexpectedly.*
7) *The amount of notice required depends on the size of the business and whether the members are scattered or all in one place.*

Directing Committee

8) *The custom is to have not less than 3 people and not more than 13, except where less than (say) a dozen members just have one director/manager.*

9) *It is quite usual to give directors a 5 year term of office. In any event they should not be constantly changed. A minimum of a year is suggested.*

Management Board

10) *The Board may comprise just one person (i.e.the general manager) or it may comprise 3 or 5 persons.*

11) *Unlike elected directors, who may be glad to retire after their period of office, managers will be professionals who look for promotion. They will expect to have high earnings grades, and it may be appropriate to give them contracts of service. Where a manager fails, and consequently has to take an inferior position at a lower earnings grade, it is better if possible for him to go to another worker-owned business.*

Works Council

12) *When there are more than (say) 50 members in a worker-owned company, the necessarily infrequent General Assembly meetings do not give the members sufficient control of their business. Hence this additional arrangement.*

Supervisory Committee

13) *The sort of thing to be checked will be directors and managers expense accounts. Here again however, this committee is only necessary as an enterprise gets larger.*

Earnings Grades

14) *Grades in Mondragon are between 10 and 30: but you may require (say) between 10 and 50 if you want to attract the best managers.*

Cash Distributions

15) *Weekly or monthly — better the latter.*

16) *Necessary until the taxation authorities begin to discover that worker-owners are self-employed business owners.*

Capital Holdings

17) *Reference the explanation in Chapter 12 and Appendix I, it is assumed that 'shareholdings' have been chosen.*

18) *It is assumed that the original members will have already allocated shareholdings to themselves, in consideration of their work in creating the business.*
19) *A complication arises if members become entitled to capital sums under ordinary law on leaving. Some skilled wording of this agreement may be required to prevent them from getting paid twice over.*
20) *To prevent people quitting just to get hold of capital.*
21) *Where a member is promoted and thus due to pay more for his increased shareholding, he must of course be given time to pay.*

Capital Valuations

22) *This sounds very difficult but will become comparatively easy once an Arbiter has discovered how to do it. Stock market analysts do it all the time.*

Amendments

23) *It is expected that members will quite frequently alter their 'rule book'.*

Interpretation

24) *If people cannot get justice from their fellow workers, then industrial democracy will fail anyhow. However, where the enterprise is a member of a group or combine, disputes can be referred to the headquarters of that body.*

Appendix K — WAGES AND PROFITS

"The cause of all these evils is the wages system. So long as we continue to work for wages: so long will we continue to be subject to the evils of which we complain" — William Sylvis, American trade union leader.

Wages

When one man is 'employed' by another man, he is paid a 'wage' in return for his work, irrespective of the results of that work. When a man is 'self-employed' he is paid a price for what he produces, irrespective of how much work he does. In the first case a man's work is controlled by his 'employer': in the second case it is controlled by himself.

These facts are well understood, as a result of which a carpenter (for example) working on his own would never describe himself as being paid 'wages'. To be self-employed and to be in receipt of wages is a contradiction in terms. Two or three self-employed carpenters might work together on a job, splitting the proceeds between them: but they would never describe these earnings as wages. They might make a notional allocation of 'wages' to themselves in their tax returns: but they would be well aware that (except as it might reduce taxation) this made no difference to their real position. If three self employed people can work together, so can 300. Worker-owners are thus self-employed persons who share (on whatever basis they may decide) their business earnings. It is not possible to be a business worker-owner and to be in receipt of 'wages', as that word is normally used and understood.

Some people argue that, since a limited liability business is a separate legal entity, it can employ and pay wages to the people who own it. However, although this may be legally correct, it has no practical significance. All the net earnings of a worker-owned business (limited or not) belong to its worker-owners: so that any cash 'paid' to them is simply part of their own money. The owners of a capitalist business are in the same position. They might contend that, since a business undertakes to pay agreed minimum wages to the people who supply it with work, it ought also to undertake to pay minimum rates of interest on the capital supplied. However, because business owners (whether workers or capitalists) already own whatever money is available, the point has no practical relevance.

Profits

The word 'profit' is well understood to mean the money remaining in hand after all legal commitments are met. In a conventional business, the capitalist owners decide how much labour they want and then enter into a legal

180

agreement to pay the required wages and salaries. The profits arise only after that commitment has been met. These profits are used to requite the capitalists both for the money they decide to supply and for their conduct of the business. In a worker-owned business (in which all externally supplied capital is borrowed) the worker-owners decide how much capital they want and then enter into a legal agreement to pay the required interest. The profits arise only after that commitment has been met. These profits are used to requite the workers both for the labour they supply and for their conduct of the business. It follows that, whereas the profits of a conventional business arise after payment of wages and salaries, the profits of a worker-owned business arise before the workers get any reward.

Practical Importance

It may be argued that all the above is just a matter of semantics. People at work require to get money every week (or month). What does it matter whether this money is called "wages" or not? Similarly, what does it matter when "profits" are deemed to arise?

The word 'wages' can seriously mislead worker-owners. In a conventional business quite a number of people exist who are concerned to see that the wages are paid. This is because, if a business fails to pay its wages, it goes bust. This damages a lot of people besides the workers. Workers who are employed by capitalists can thus normally rely on the capitalist owners to see that they get their weekly cash. In a worker-owned business by contrast, no one beyond the workers themselves is concerned with ensuring that money will be available for their cash drawings. If the workers do not worry about it, they can be sure that no one else will.

It has been pointed out that capitalist business owners gain nothing by having an agreement with their business for any fixed interest payment on their equity shares, because whatever business earnings may be available belong to them anyhow. Suppose that a conventional company was 'floated' on the stock exchange and that its 'ordinary' shares were offered with a commitment by the company to pay a minimum rate of interest on them. The promoters would be charged with fraud (and possibly imprisoned) on the grounds that they were inducing people to buy shares by offering a supposed advantage, which could not in fact exist. Similarly, anyone who induces people to start a worker-owned enterprise on the basis of its members being paid wages is guilty of fraud!

Avoidance of the word wages has other advantages. A trade union official at a conference is recorded as saying that "unions may sometimes need to to allow new cooperatives to pay less wages than those agreed with large companies". That kind of misconception would not arise if it was made clear that worker-owners, so far from being paid wages, merely draw out of their business some of their own money.

The word 'profits' (used without explanation) can seriously mislead those concerned with taxation of worker-owned businesses. It may be thought that, if taxation is levied on the 'surplus' remaining after worker-owners have made their regular cash drawings, the practical effect will be that of a normal 'profits tax'. However this is not so, because worker-owners can always reduce a surplus by drawing out more cash, which they can return to their business later as a gift. No tax authorities yet worry about this problem: but they will have to do so as worker-ownership increases. The solution is of course to re-define the word 'profits' in regard to worker-owned businesses and to charge a much lower rate of profits tax on such enterprises.

Misunderstanding of the word 'profits' also helps to mislead worker-owners themselves, because they also tend to equate it with the surplus remaining at the end of the year. They thus fail to see that the amount of this surplus depends, at least in part, on the rate of cash drawings which they decide. As explained under 'Cash Drawings' in Chapter 12, these should be decided in the light of a forecast, firstly of the business earnings, and secondly of the amount of those earnings required for re-investment.*

*The following illustrates the danger of worker-owners getting used to drawing out regular fixed sums of money. The Mondragon organisers took great care NOT to use the term wages, for which they substituted the word *anticipos* (meaning an anticipation of the business earnings). However the members of the Mondragon enterprises agreed to limit their cash drawings to the equivalent of local wages, in order to create capital which would provide more jobs for fellow Basques. As the first enterprise (Ulgor) was very successful, it always made far more than was required to pay out the equivalent of local wages, and its members thus became accustomed to making cash drawings at that level. However, after about 20 years, their particular industry suffered a big depression, which faced the members with hard times for a period. At their General Meeting in 1980 it was proposed to the members that it would be prudent for them to take a lower rate of cash drawings *(anticipos)* than usual for the ensuing year. However the members had become so used to getting the local rate of wages that they had come to regard it as a 'minimum' amount of cash, and the General Meeting voted against the proposal. It was not until 1981 that the members could be got to face up to the facts, by which time an even bigger reduction was required. It is nice to record that the business was then saved and has since returned to prosperity.

Appendix L — TRADE UNIONS

"All violent feelings produce in us a falseness in our impressions of external things" — John Ruskin

It is explained in Chapter 1 how the new factories of the industrial revolution altered the balance of power between employers and employed, so that it became necessary for workers to combine in 'unions'. However this need disappears when workers become both employers and employed. The point was well put by a member of the Czechoslovakian workers cooperative organisation, when he said: "Why would cooperative members want trade unions, when they elect their own business leaders?" Why indeed? As explained in Chapter 7, trade unions are like crutches used by a man with a bad leg. While his leg is bad they are the essential to him, because he would be immobile without them: but, when his leg is healed, the crutches are no longer needed. Similarly with trade unions. They are essential in conventional industry: but in worker-ownership conditions they serve no purpose.

It must not however be thought that trade unions will necessarily cease to exist. Large long established organisations do not suddenly disappear. Trade Unions may gradually run down, but they may also change their role. For example, there is always a danger of democratic organisations becoming 'institutionalised'. One possible role for trade unions is that of watch dogs for industrial democracy.

Trade unions have a long and great tradition of championing the cause of working people. It would thus be imagined that the keenest promoters of worker-ownership would be trade union officials. Here is the happy ending to 150 years of effort to free workers from the thraldom of capital. What better solution can there be than one which makes workers (instead of capitalists) the owners of industry? Worker-ownership should surely be the summit of every trade unionist's ambition. There may be difficulties in achieving the change-over from capital ownership: but it is trade unionists who should be keenest to overcome them. However this is not so.

The writer well remembers how people felt at the end of the last war against the Germans. At that point in time, had anyone proposed an alliance of France and Britain with Germany, he would have been looked on as a lunatic. Out of the previous thirty years, nearly ten years had been spent at war with Germany: and, as always happens in war, 'the enemy' had been represented as villains of the deepest dye. People in France and Britain would have found it emotionally impossible to consider the idea of Germans as allies. Looking back now it is difficult to recall the force of the feelings which then existed and which clouded any rational judgement. Germany was the great danger against which all sensible Frenchmen and Britons must be on their guard. At that time the idea of ceasing to maintain arms against Germany would have been unthinkable.

Consider then the position of trade unionists. They have been fighting against capitalists, not for ten, but for 150 years. As far back as even their great grandfathers could remember, it has been the object of trade unions to protect their members from capitalists. They have been taught (as always in a war) that capitalists are naturally bad people. To be a 'capitalist' is something of which any right minded citizen ought to be ashamed. Then along comes someone like the writer of this book, who says: ''You can disband your trade union army: it won't be needed any more. We can arrange for your members to avoid control by capitalists. Indeed we're going to make your members into capitalists themselves. You must help us promote this beautiful new world in which the 'two sides' of industry will disappear.''

Is it surprising that most trade unionists dismiss the whole idea out of hand, without even enquiring into its detail?

Appendix M — FULL EMPLOYMENT

"The proof of the pudding is in the eating" — Trad.

People raised in the conventional capital ownership system (which is all of us) find it difficult to believe in the possibility of business enterprises which never 'go bust'. It is therefore relevant to give examples of what happens in practice, and to consider the problem in further detail.

Help Available

It is in the nature of human endeavour that, however good a system may be, a minority of people will make a muddle of it. This was exemplified by a member of the headquarters staff of the Hungarian workers' co-operatives, who said to the author "of course we expect to have three or four problem cooperatives each year". The Hungarian added that they had in the past found it easiest to deal with a 'problem' cooperative by arranging for it to amalgamate with a prosperous one in the same line of business. However, as in Poland, it had been found that this resulted in many enterprises becoming too large: so that other arrangements are now made. It will be appreciated that, although the Hungarian government uses state funds to solve any problems arising in state enterprises, the workers' co-operative organisation is expected to solve its own problems with its own resources.

The point which this illustrates is that worker-owned businesses have a natural feeling of responsibility for each other: so that a group of such enterprises will always rescue one of their number in difficulty. The members of that enterprise will never be left to suffer 'redundancy' or (in Eastern Europe) to having to accept employment by the state

Historical Evidence

In 1977 the author was discussing with an English banker the Mondragon policy of never letting a business go into liquidation. The banker said "such a policy may be possible now: but the Mondragon organisation would never be able to maintain it in face a major business recession." Ten years later in 1987, when these words are being written, history has proved the banker to have been mistaken.

A major business recession was in fact already taking shape in Spain in 1977. This was foreseen by the Management Division of the Mondragon Bank, who issued a general warning to the member enterprises of the group that they should endeavour to increase or create exports. However the trade recession which first hit Spain then went on to affect the whole industrial world: so that the Mondragon Group had no escape. Thus for example Ulgor,

185

the first and biggest of the cooperatives, which had regularly increased its output over the previous ten years, suddenly found half its production lines idle as its markets disappeared. All the Mondragon enterprises felt the draught, to a greater or lesser degree. What happened?

One result was of course that the Mondragon members got less money, both in cash drawings and in capital accretion. However no member received less cash than 80% of his or her previous normal rate. Some members drew this as unemployment benefit, paid by the Mondragon welfare organisation: but, even at the height of the recession, unemployment never exceeded 2%. Further, unemployment of individuals was never more than temporary.

It need hardly be said that enormous problems had to be overcome. However a number of members were able to move from enterprises in a particularly bad way to others able to employ them: and a number were required to accept retirement at 60. In general, the Mondragon group proved its ability to ride out a world business recession without business failures or serious redundancy.

Rather sadly, it was found expedient to abandon the record that no Mondragon enterprise had ever closed its doors. Closure was applied to eight small businesses, with a total of 250 members. However this was little more than 'the exception which proves the rule'. In a group of some 20,000 people, it was easier to find other enterprises willing to take on the members concerned than to revive these small ailing businesses.

It was also necessary to accept some failure to repay loans. This applied to the small businesses above, and to failures to make full repayment of loans by some other enterprises in the group. However the sums involved were a fraction of the total loans involved and comprised losses which the Bank* could easily absorb. The group was thus able to meet all its commitments to the public, from whom the money was originally borrowed. Here again therefore was an 'exception which proves the rule' that a group headquarters staff is able to lend money to member enterprises in circumstances in which it will always be repaid.

Special Cases

Mondragon is a mixed group formed on a geographical basis, in which circumstances even a world depression does not affect all the different businesses equally. However it has been explained (under 'Unemployment' in Chapter 16) that worker-ownership groups are more likely to operate on a trade basis: and a widespread depression in the trade of such a group might have an even more severe effect. Thus for example a group of worker-owned

*The Mondragon group is certainly helped by having a Savings Bank which consistently makes profits. However the Bank only makes profits by lending to the enterprises at slightly higher rates than would otherwise be necessary. Any money used to write off loans thus comes eventually from all the other borrowers within the group.

186

businesses producing steel in the late 1970s might have found it impossible to keep all its members in receipt of reasonable amounts of cash. There are two answers to such a situation.

One is that worker-owners are much less likely to get caught in such circumstances, because of the policy of placing security of employment above maximisation of earnings (see the fourth para under 'Commercial Viability' in Chapter 11). A group of worker-owned steel producers would thus have been unlikely to have joined in the general expansion of steel production which ended in the collapse of the market.

The other answer is that, where a market disappears in circumstances which nobody could have foreseen, a group of worker-owners can reasonably turn to their fellow citizens for help — as explained under 'Exceptional Circumstances' in Chapter 16.

Postscript

"Before I became a Minister in the government, I used to think how difficult it must be to decide on the right national policies. I find in practice that it is comparatively easy to know what to do: the difficulty is to get people to do it." — Lord Chandos, during a lecture in 1943.

It is the theme of this book, not just that worker-ownership of business enterprises is a better system than conventional capital-ownership, but that, until we achieve industrial democracy, industrial and social disharmony will continue. This was the picture being unfolded in the Western world during most of the first half of the 20th century: so that, by the 1970s, industrial disputes had become a normal occurrence. The forecast made in 1924 of increasing trouble in production, which is quoted at the end of Appendix C, was being steadily borne out.

However this book is being published at a time when Mr Reagan in the U.S.A., Mrs Thatcher in Britain and Mr Gorbachev in Russia have initiated a period of turning back from Left wing economic theory. It may thus be thought that the majority of people have decided to abandon Left wing policies and to accept the need for 'sensible' arrangements. This, in the author's opinion, is to ignore the phenomenon of (what is called in Britain) the Militant Left. These people cannot just be written off as a lunatic fringe. They comprise too big a minority of most of the developed nations. (The literature of the Institute for Workers Control in Britain can be found as far apart as Stockholm in Sweden and Boston in America.) There must be some reason for the existence of these people and for the degree of support they receive.

A reason commonly put forward is envy. They are seen as representing the less able members of society, who envy their more successful fellow citizens and thus demand policies which will provide them with the money they fail to earn for themselves. No doubt this is a factor: but it is not an adequate explanation of the phenomenon. If the 20th century has seen a rise in industrial dissatisfaction, it has also seen an enormous rise in industrial prosperity. The citizens of the developed nations are all very much better off than they were 50 years ago: and yet a substantial minority of them vociferously complain.

This is contrary to what we normally observe in human nature. People may suffer injustice and may rebel against it: but they do not do so at a time when their lot is improving. The rebellion comes only when there is some set-back in their material progress. Then their latent dissatisfaction surfaces and they

188

demand change, if necessary with violence. What then is it which motivates substantial numbers of people to join in extreme Left wing demands today? The answer was given by William Straker (see 'Industrial Slavery' in Chapter 2) when he said that "the root of the matter is the straining of the spirit of man to be free". The underlying cause of dissatisfaction is lack of industrial democracy.

It is thus a mistake to assume that we may now expect an era of calm. Trouble will come back again. Therefore, although it may seem to us unnecessary to worry about implementing worker-ownership, and although it may appear much easier just to let things go on as they are, we do not really have that option. Action of some kind will, sooner or later, be forced upon us.

Unfortunately Left wing activity tends to centre on trade unionism: and Appendix L explains how very difficult it is for trade unions to see that their own demise, within a system of worker-ownership, is what their members really need. The danger then is that the wrong reforms are again attempted: so that, in due course, we have to suffer further periods of bad economic and social policies. Better to initiate the right change now.